Letters from "An Unknown Writer"

Grace E. Cote

DORRANCE PUBLISHING CO., INC.
PITTSBURGH, PENNSYLVANIA 15222

ISBN: 978-1-4349-0259-7
Library of Congress Control Number: 2008934694

Printed in the United States of America

First Printing

For more information or to order additional books, please contact:
Dorrance Publishing Co., Inc.
701 Smithfield Street
Pittsburgh, Pennsylvania 15222
U.S.A.
1-800-788-7654
www.dorrancebookstore.com

Dedication

To Rebekkah, Mark, and Paul, my awesome children, who are the greatest joy in my life.

For sharing themselves and for sharing their gifts, for being my coach, and for being my earthly savior, to:

Michael S. Greevy, Ph.D.
Kurtis D. Jens, M.D.
Paul M. Epstein, M.D.

I thank, rejoice, and sing to my God, creator, redeemer, sustainer.

Table of Letters

Introduction

For everything there is a season, and a time for every matter under heaven:

> a time to be born, and a time to
>   die;
> a time to plant, and a time to
>   pluck up what is planted;
> a time to kill, and a time to heal;
> a time to break down, and a time to
>   build up;
> a time to weep, and a time to
>   laugh;
> a time to mourn, and a time to
>   dance;
> a time to throw away stones, and a time to
>   gather stones
>   together;
> a time to embrace, and a time to
>   refrain from embracing;
> a time to seek, and a time to lose;
> a time to keep, and a time to
>   throw away;
> a time to tear, and a time to sew,
> a time to keep silence, and a time
>   to speak
> a time to love, and a time to hate;
> a time for war, and a time for
>   peace.

Ecclesiastes 3:1-8

to an unknown publisher—

I ask myself, "Could you be interested in reading my letters?" Of all the letters I've written, this one has proven to be the most difficult. I feel the burden is on me to prove something to you, which I can't. My letters will have to talk for themselves. They will have to sing their own melody.

I've been emboldened to submit them for your consideration by my soulful presence. He has read my letters. His responses to my letters and his feedback encouraged me to send my letters to you, "unknown publisher." He and I believe they are worthy enough to invite your interest. I'm swept up in the ecstasy that I could write well enough and at the same time could tap the imagination of others.

My soulful presence knows me. Mike and I have a relationship. We talk together. We share our thoughts and feelings together. We cry. We laugh. We are serious when we need to be serious. When he reads my letters, I feel excited. His enthusiasm energizes me, but would my letters have meaning to anyone else besides mike?

My letters are based on my 68 years of experiences. I have my own slant on life, and yet what I write about, I think, joins me with my "unknown readers." We are united one with another. We have times of fun. We have times of laughter. We have times of anger. We think. We feel. We have times of seriousness. We all strive for something. We all feel pain. We all hope. We are all bound in this thing called life. We have commonality.

My trek has included many helpers. From my relationship with mike, my letters were born. Through years of therapy, I kept a journal. When the letters magically began, my thrust changed from writing for myself to writing for others, to touch others as others have touched me along the way. Some might say I have an impossible dream. I seek to reach another's soul by opening mine. I use the letter format because it is more personal, and I can break some grammatical rules. I don't think readers are worried about format, syntax, or composition correctness. One theme that can be found throughout my letters is that I ask a lot of questions. I don't always find the answers, but I continue to ask, continue to seek, and I invite my "unknown readers" to ask, to seek, in order to find. We are all in this quest together. A big question remains, "Can unknown readers identify with my walk?" Do the letters transcend one person's life?

With humility, I send my letters. Regardless of the outcome of this action, my pen and paper bearing my words are sufficient to cause me delight. The writing process, in and of itself, causes me to rejoice. Do I have a special gift? Would the letters make a difference? I don't know the answer to any of the questions in this letter, so it is with gratitude I share my written words with you. Whatever your reaction, "unknown publisher," I'm content knowing I'm already published in my little corner of the world.

with inherent joy,
"an unknown writer"

Any time
Any day

Dearest Rebekkah, Paul, and Mark—

A large core issue in my life has become clearer through my intense work with doc. epstein, doc. jens, and now, doc. mike. I have struggled for such a long time to be able to forgive others and loved ones especially, but harder than that is the ability to forgive myself.

The area I want to share with you—Rebekkah, Paul, and Mark—is the early years of my illness, continuing in Portland, till all of you graduated from college. (The journey goes on, but I have worked very hard to use therapy for improvement and transitions to health. My only regret is you guys were not around to benefit from my process.) I want to give you some background information to help clarify the situation. I was misdiagnosed and was put on the wrong medications. I didn't stabilize nor get better. The psychiatrist I had was so afraid I would commit suicide on "his watch," he overreacted when my feelings of despair surfaced. He quickly admitted me into psych hospitals. My hospitalizations became a revolving door since I was despairing a lot at that time. Sadly, during that time of treatment, 60-day stays were the norm because insurance companies covered it (so there were 60-day *cures*). This practice was not therapeutic. I became dependent on the mental health system and actually regressed. (Today, hospitalizations are only days and only an option in specific cases—being a danger to

3

oneself or others.) These were the realities, which you may or may not have known back then.

But, primarily, I'm writing to you to tell you how I felt, and still feel, about these facts in my relationship with you. I am so sad that I hurt you. I was never really able to tell you that I didn't act out or purposely want to cause you harm, and that it was never your fault. It was the disorder, "broken brain." However, this information doesn't address how you felt about it all. It couldn't stop feelings you may have had, such as confusion, insecurity, fear, abandonment, aloneness, helplessness, and others. I had, and still have, a deep regret for what I did and didn't do to you during this time. I still have a heavy heart and years of tears over it. I want to leave the gloomy haunts of sadness. I want to forgive myself for those chaotic times. I have been waiting for your forgiveness, even though that stance misses the point. I have to do the work of forgiveness for myself, so I've decided I need to take another course.

I want to forgive myself now so I can let the past go. I've discovered guilt is not a good motivator for my actions or decisions. Like in AA, one of the steps to recovery is to make amends to those you've wronged or hurt. I want to tell you how sorry I am for the crazy, chaotic years you experienced with me. My prayer is that by telling you this, I can feel less condemnatory towards myself and begin the healing process. I realize those troubled years were a long time ago, but I still carry feelings about how this period of your life was most difficult for you, and I was the cause. I've come to realize I have to learn how to forgive myself in regard to our past experiences together. Rationally, I know I was ill and had no control over that, but on a feeling level, I still feel pained about how all of this impacted your young lives.

I'm hoping by saying, "I'm sorry," in the here and now will prevent accumulating heaps of more guilt. In the present, I can tell you how sorry I am when I say or do hurtful things. I'm grateful I can be aware enough to realize when I have been offensive to you. I'm exalted knowing a mom—me—can apologize to her kids—you. It is good I can show you that I made and make mistakes still. You can see my "not okay," my "not so nice" parts. Of course, you have always known that, but it is also important I accept that about myself, too. To learn I don't have to go through life beating myself up for not being perfect, or that I bruised others, including you three. To know I don't have to seek penitence for all my transgressions and never find relief. That I can trust God's grace is sufficient. The mother of the past doesn't work anymore. You—Rebekkah, Paul, and Mark—are autonomous beings and so grown up. How delightful it is we can relate in deeper and more mature places, with no functioning roles or labels. I'm willing to take the risk to tell you how sorrowful I am when I invade your boundaries, for by doing so, I honor your dignity and personhood. How wonderful that course is to take.

As this letter attests to my regrets and guilt, unfortunately they can still be tapped. I know full well they can still haunt me. Perhaps my progress in therapy will never completely cut through or loosen the bedrock feelings I have about the past with you—Rebekkah, Mark, and Paul. My guilt gets triggered again when my actions in the todays cause injury to you or others, but at least I can make things right now. I have the courage to share how my behaviors are wrongful and can ask you to forgive me. Then, I hope, I can let my guilty feelings go, that I don't have to store them up for years, as I have done in the past (26 years is a very long time). Right now I'm in an awesome place. With God's help, and mike's, I'm now working towards forgiveness, which also brings the prospect of inner peace, and as always, I want you—Rebekkah, Mark, and Paul—to know how deeply I love you. (I always did, but it didn't show as much then.) It is marvelous to be able to say I'm sorry to you, on one hand, and on the other, be freed up to forgive myself. Funny how it works that way. You continue to be a blessing to me, and I thank God for the gifts of you—Rebekkah, Paul, and Mark—every day.

Love you lots,

Mom

planet earth

to a known stranger—

"What's in a name?" You have a name, I just don't know it; but I'm writing to you from a place of commonality: that of being human.

I have struggled a long time to get my life together. At times it felt like I was fighting windmills, but some small voice told me to keep the course, to girdle up, to win the battle for healing, transformation, and new birth. Hearing the words of my psychiatrist about my prognosis, "You will end up in a back ward in a state hospital," started a journey from hell. There were years of tears, pain, confusion, cursing the moon, suicide attempts, feeling like a piece of shit. Rocking in a corner, sobbing, "Where is my deliverance?"

From a bad beginning, I came to be awed when I realized I had been led along the way by many "helpers" (professionals and common folk like us). And the irony is I would never had come to know them if I had not embarked on my mental health journey. In time I let them into my crazy world and bleak sojourn. I went from a snake pit to a mansion; from feeling stupid to knowledge; from disbelief to trust; from isolation to inclusion; from being blocked to openness; from having feet of clay to dancing; from being blind to seeing; from despair to hope. I was dragged from dark to light. I now see beauty and awe in myself, others, the world. TO BE: Alive! Aware! Insightful! Exhilarated! Compassionate! I feel heady, intoxicated with life. Sometimes I don't know what to make of it all or how to contain it, if that is even necessary. I feel like the psalmist's song, "My cup runneth over." There is so much to learn, to do, to feel. I want to embrace life, not just exist or be bogged down with the details, bane things in our lives. There has to be more than accomplishments, degrees, titles, or money in living. Do you think we humans find it so much easier to work towards these goals rather than change direction and go inside to find our souls? Is that too alarming? The quest doesn't come with a price tag. Everyone can afford it; everyone can have it. It merely takes a backpack full of trail mix, willingness, and courage. Can we embark on this adventure together?

Something marvelous is happening. We all have the power to be transformed into something new. Granted, we all are unique individuals, but what joy there would be if we can join up with other journeyers and share the gift of life. It would be fantastic if we all had the ability to leave footprints on others' souls. We have both the choice and opportunity in our joint search for meaning. What is the purpose of our walk on the sands of time? Whatever it is, wouldn't it be easier if we held hands? The decision is up to us, but our choices will affect others anyway. If by reading my words you can view your feelings or understandings in a different way, if you should be touched by them, then I'm touched. Hi, soulful friend. Let's face it—we need each other, and that fact is not a weakness or sentimentality. I jump on happy feet knowing I might find new fellow travelers to come with me on a new divergent path.

I don't know about you, but I choose to try to engage others, even if it is only for a few minutes. I want to let them know they matter to me, that we are bound to each other just by being part of the human race. I feel very lonely if I can't reach out and make connections with someone else. It doesn't always work, but my batting average is up there. At least I risked. I still invite, invite. I believe others yearn for the human touch, no matter how brief, small, or simple. Can we unlatch the shackles that keep us imprisoned in our damp, dark dungeons? Locked away from seeing that we can be a conduit for mending, peace, and liberty? May we be blessed with moments of "ahas"? May we be so lucky? Then we can walk in an attitude of gratitude.

A reminder—the ocean was created before time and will continue beyond our lives, so we don't have forever "to get it." We tend to want to build barriers between us, to keep us divided and separated; to look at the world going by, hidden unto ourselves. Rather, let our actions be liken to gleefully opening a gaily wrapped present, a gift celebrating us. So, world, make way for us. We are on the march, unique and the same.

Oh! What delight! Because worldly goods, the tangibles that are so important to us, could be stripped away, but the human soul is eternal.

The point of writing all this to you is to encourage you to join me in shouting up to the rooftops, up to the heavens. I guess we first have to realize that being in our own place and space needs to be extended to include all those other people out there. There really are signs in reality that we have the possibility to love one another. Ode to compassion! You know, even if we deny it, we *are* a part of the family of men and women. We need to remember that we are *only* a part of the human history, of the human story. So let's make that story a best seller.

Whatever your name, whatever the name of the place you live, we are linked. I've shared my story with you, from hopelessness to rejoicing. You also have a story to tell, to share. By reaching out to you in this letter, my words have shattered silence.

You don't know my name, but you know me.

from one explorer to another explorer

to a congregation in nowheresville—

Let me introduce myself. I'm The Reverend David Cote's wife. Pretty daunting, wouldn't you say? In later years, he was called "The Rev." I guess then I was Mrs. "The Rev." It wasn't always that way. I actually had an identity once. I'll tell you, it's tough being a title, a role, stereotypcd. I was boxed in by you church members. I was put into a plain, drab, ugly box, which no one wanted to open. You would stick Post-its on it with any description that suited you. You pasted my box with labels that had nothing to do with the contents. The only times you let me out, you still demanded I be what you wanted me to be. Dragged from my dilapidated box, only when you needed to expose my failures, to point your fingers at me, to find something you could criticize. The biggest prize for you was when you could blame me for all the wrong things going on in your lives.

For 41 years I had to be what I'm not. I needed to force your myths onto myself and to live up to your perceptions 24/7. When you acted this way, it was hard to trust you. I got confused when you said hi with a smiling face and then gossiped about me later with scorn. Your standards for me were so much higher than yours were for you. I got confused with the church being called the "body of Christ," a faith community. Your words and actions bespoke of the world's values rather than being disciples of Jesus Christ, ambassadors to others. Are we not invited to live our lives spreading the "good news" of the Gospel? It's not about offering feel-good messages to the world, which then confuses the "good news" with "pleasant news." I will never say that this task is easy. Don't you think we could at least work at it? We sure aren't perfect people or perfect church members. Only God, our creator and redeemer, has that job. This is why we daily confess our sins. It's too marvelous for words; we actually get forgiven day after day.

It is imperative we take our acts of worship back into our needy world. It seems to me all our hymns of praise, liturgies, scripture lessons, sharing the peace, and the Eucharist don't stop when we say, "Amen, alleluia." We all know when the service is over, but it isn't over until the minister says, "Go in peace and serve the Lord." Do we forget the serving part? Oh, there you go again.

"Oh, the sermon was too long."

"Oh, the choir sang off-key."

"Oh, all those restless noisy kids."

"Didn't she wear that get-up last Sunday?"

"Oh, the service went over the sacred, holy sixty minutes."

Do you think God is watching His wristwatch? He might be checking how many minutes we offer up our praises to Him. All of our sacraments, baptism, and Holy Communion, attest to Christ's intent for us, His loving forgiveness freely given. Actually, we have two altars. The first is made of marble, stone, or wood. Those altars are in safe, comfortable havens. We see them from our familiar pews. The other altar is a living altar. At this altar, we make our offerings to God too, but it is expressed in service to our brothers and sisters. Our love of God is expressed through our actions, not just our words. It's hard to understand that in 2000 years, we still don't get it, for St. Peter's sake. We continue to bring our grudges, anger, and singular pronouns (I) to our houses of worship. We hear forgiveness, but we don't forgive. Let's not have our joyful hymns of praise go flat, discordant. Can we relate with each other as conjoined souls? Aren't we all worthy of each other's forgiveness and love? Can we accept others just as they are, not how we want them to be? I promise, if you don't judge me, I won't judge you.

You, congregational members, in all the times I was hospitalized, you didn't come. Dave came for short visits, but I was pissed at him anyway. With all the scary sounds and sights in a psych hospital, my children refused to come at all. I desperately needed your support and caring. I was hurting very badly. Being alone to face this world alone is impossible, excruciating. Congregations, being as fickle and as human as they are, in my role I couldn't have favorites (even though I did in my heart). Having church members as friends was unthinkable; it wasn't an option (for fear of jealousy). I'm wondering if by now you are getting the themes of my existence? Can you connect the dots...dots...dots...dots...? Can you guys be with me? Can you surround me? Hold me? This is a two-way street. I will be there for you, making connections with you. Let's make a pledge. We can show our real selves; we can show others how real we are, in all our human ways, and never let go. Hold up high banners that proclaim, "WE CARE. WE ARE SENSITIVE TO OTHERS' NEEDS."

As Dave's spouse, I saw him "bigger than life." He was a community icon. His favorite place was the ER in our community hospital. He led worship services most Sundays of the year; he preached; he taught; he counseled; he visited; he went to all meetings and programs of the church (I had to do some of that too); he did tons of paperwork; he performed baptisms, weddings, funerals (he would officiate at funeral services for non-members as well). He became chaplain of both the fire and police departments. He received the "Citizen of the Year" award. He won so many awards he was running out of room on the walls of the parsonage to hang them. Being a member of the Mass Corps of Fire Chaplains, he was deployed to *Ground Zero* (2x) shortly after the attacks. Phew! It must make sense to you by now why I was alone a lot. The kids and I weren't very high on Dave's priorities list. We got lost in the shuffle by Dave's bigger ministry of being in the world, outer directed. The kids are PKs (pastor's kids), so the terms of engagement applied to them as well. Perhaps writing about my kids will be a letter for another day. With all of Dave's accomplishments, I paled. I asked myself, *Who the hell do you think you are? You could never reach those heights. What do you have to offer?* I'm a nobody, not even a documented immigrant. I have no passport to enter this strange land. Where do I go from here?

In good time, I found my way. I determined life is more than plaques on a wall somewhere. I decided to take a journey into the recessed depths of who I am—my soul. I am so grateful that by being a pastor's wife, I found myself right in the core of life's cycles, right there, "down and dirty," with all sorts of people trying to figure out what it's all about, too. We have rather large burlap bags of goodies to share. I like burlap bags. They have an earthy smell. Can we join in song? Can we sing, fiddle, whistle, chant, hum, beat drums, clash symbols? Can the whole earth be plucked like a stringed instrument? What a choir of myriad sounds that would be. There is a beat; there is a rhythm. All of us are at the heart of the melody, and be assured, it wouldn't take a whole lot of practice, either. We already know the lines; we are all virtuosos. Let our cacophony of music come together from our hearts.

Then there was the dying. As a pastor's wife, I was involved in the heights and depths of living. I was there when there were sorrows. I was there when there were doubts. I was there when there was illness. I was there for the questions. I was there for the contradictions in life that made no sense. I was touched by their lives. I loved them. They were my "family." Funerals were the worst, an experience of pain and suffering. I went to more funerals than "the average bear." There were so many of them. One year there were 22 funeral services. Some funerals left indelible lacerations on my heart. Some funerals were not as terrible—those for the very old, or hopelessly sick. I didn't have to use my Kleenex as much. Then there were the funerals that were horrendous deaths: the young, the very young, fatal accidents (of all kinds), suicides, ODs, murders, fires, drownings, and bodies that suddenly stopped working. We even had a school shooting, long before it became a common happening.

My mother used to tell me I was "too sensitive." With all the bad things that happened to my "family," maybe she was right. There were unforgettable wounds on my soul. My faith told me of Christ's redeeming acts, giving us eternal life, by His victory over death. Yeah, give me a break. What do I do with these empty feelings? People in my life leave me behind. They are gone from my presence, my reality. There is a big ache there, a deep, deep longing.

There is one memory that still pierces my heart and always will. A house across the street was engulfed in flames one night. The mother finally jumped from the second floor window after many shouts from the fireman telling her to do it. Her two young sons died in the intense blaze. The morning after there was nothing recognizable. I really couldn't believe appliances melt. The scene became a monument for a charred shell, silence and suffering, to the highest degree. There were smoky tears for the loss of two young lives. They never had a chance—an unspeakable horror. The red-orange flames mixed with black/gray smoke lit up a despairing night. There is something to a burned smell. It can't be forgotten. There was debris all around. The hardest for me was seeing a little sneaker on the lawn. It was red. Such excruciating anguish. Such woe. In the mother's jumping, she shattered bones in her feet and legs. She faced a very long time in rehab for her body to heal. At the same time, she had to mourn the loss of her sons. How does one deal with extreme body pain and extreme psych pain at the same time? What an emotional roller coaster. I think you can guess which one would be the most difficult to do.

Then there was John. He lived down the street from us. He was friends with my kids. One summer he went to camp. I'm sure he expected to have fun and new learning experiences. John came home in a box. He was only 15. He died while he was using ropes and pulleys to slide himself across a chasm. John was not a member of our church, but we had the biggest one in town. It was standing room only. The penetrating grief in the air permeated our parched throats, making it difficult to breathe and sing. John's family never really rebounded from his tragic, untimely death. Eventually, John's mother, father, brother, and sister sold their house and moved away. It's too bad changing geography really won't erase all the contusions in our soul. They will be etched into our very fibers. How does a parent deal with not being able to talk with his or her kid ever again? Not be able to love him, not be able to hug him, not be able to listen to him, not to be able to see his life unfold? His parents will never see him again. How would we handle such grief? How would we deal with our own denial, anger, and immense loss? Is it possible to come to an acceptance place? I know if my kids die before me, I would become a member of the "walking dead club." Losing my kids is my only fear in life.

I know being a pastor's wife, I was privileged and blessed. I was able to be in the trenches with others, intensively, and with great depth. I could be with other human beings in their needs and times of fun and laughter. I wasn't ready to be a pastor's wife, but I'm so glad it happened to me. I learned so much from others. My head and soul are still full of their images and their stories left in my inner core. All of a sudden, in the middle of what I've been writing about, I got these awful thoughts. I hope I haven't lost you, readers. I hope you aren't saying, "I have more important things to do." I don't blame you for thinking that way. A lot of this letter is serious. A lot of this time in my life was too serious. I didn't have a clue about balance. I didn't know about beauty, awe, or joy. The lesson I had to learn, and maybe you too, is that life is a potpourri of choices. We are in charge of our attitudes. So, let's put on shiny black tap shoes, with satin bows, and stand side by side in a chorus line of understanding and unity. Click, click, click, toe and heel. With our frolicking, fancy dancing shoes on, we can make a great noise and "bring down the house." The introduction to my letters bespeaks to this issue—"For everything there is a season, and a time for every matter under heaven." Life is more than serious. Thank God! And, let's remember not to take ourselves too seriously, either!

I climbed out of that box which imprisoned me for so long. I'm emancipated. Now I have a soulful presence in my life. His name is mike. I see him twice a week. You might be thinking the extra time must mean she is really sick. Not so, I'm very well. He has taught me so much. He inspired me. He helped me realize my words matter, my feelings matter. He helped me realize I can reach out to other kindred souls through written words. I don't have to be afraid to share my journey with your journey. If I can touch your spirit, my spirit will be touched also. This sounds like a good deal to me. I have a lot more to say about mike—more about our relationship, friendship, and sharing who we are with each other. That will have to wait for another letter. Mom was right—I am "too sensitive"—and that is something to celebrate. It's a gift—a gift I'm willing to share with you.

Peace!

Amen! (so be it)

Footnote: Dave and I made a mutual decision to get divorced. It was finalized on September 7, 2004. The court papers said we had an irretrievable breakdown. If I knew our marriage was *that* bad, I would have split a long time ago.

Ph.D.

to a known therapist—

Almost two year ago in June, I walked into mike's office for the first time. It certainly looked weird to me. All those stones, rocks, crystals, a magic wand, a container of sand, a coral with a delicate pink shell embedded underneath, and more. All in varied colors and shapes. They were all methodically positioned with great care. This certainly wasn't an office I'd ever seen before. All his props. I wondered how he used them, or were they just for effect? Then I saw mike. He had sandy-colored hair, on the long side. He had a sandy-colored goatee, mixed with gray. (I never understood why men's beards go gray first.) His stature was slender. He seemed to me to be a therapist I'd never known before nor could understand. I had a preconceived notion that Ph.D. psychologists have to be flakes, certainly not like my former psychiatrists. Having seen them for such a long time, I knew what to expect from them. My first decision was *I don't know if I can work with this guy*, and yet, with all these observations, I've never felt such a bond as I did in that first 50-minute meeting with mike. He blew me away. I couldn't figure out how it happened. To start with, all my negative thoughts and the fact I didn't even know him, it was bizarre. I don't know why, but I decided I wanted to work with him then and there. Normally I would expect to take some time to build rapport and trust, but how did it click so quickly?

After a fruitless search to find a new therapist, I found Mike's name on a list my son had printed out for me. Originally I counted him out because he was not a psychiatrist. As far as I knew, they were the only type of clinicians that could help me with my deep, deep problems. What do Ph.D.'s know when it comes to therapy? Or more importantly, what don't they know? Would it be a big risk if I decided to see mike? Could he help me? Was he a "hippie"? He sure looked like one. You're not going to believe this—he actually looked like John Lennon. But when I think about it, he looked more like Ringo Starr. Was he stuck in the 60s? Was he into "turn on, tune in, drop out" or "flower power"? Maybe I had to see him. He might have been my last resort. That thought put me in a tizzy. Was mike my last chance to find a helper? Yeeks! There was a lot riding on this Greevy guy.

I was coming from the untimely death of my psychiatrist. I felt extreme pain over this loss. I brought all my baggage to that first session. I didn't believe I could find another therapist again like doc. jens. I brought all my frustrations about having to find someone to replace him. Also, I missed not having the support I needed from a therapeutic relationship. Is this mike going to be sugary and superficial? I'm expecting a lot from you, mike. With all of these impediments, how did something special happen in that first 50-minute session? It was both magical and baffling. As of late, I sing, "How did I get so lucky?" Since I met mike, it is a lingering melody. It has become my new mantra. How freed up I feel. I would never have imagined how awesome it was to be with mike. I never imagined how much mike was going to teach me. I never thought I would be able to trust mike in that very first appointment.

Mike was never threatened as I talked on end about doc. jens. In time, he helped me from my mourning to some peace. I admire mike for listening to my grief. I told him I wasn't trying to replicate doc. jens, but I was. I'm so happy that mike was so confident and secure in himself. Then I could be comfortable in talking about another therapist, and mike was still who he was. By his example, I came to see mike as a unique, unequaled human being. I stopped seeing him and his office things as a barrier. Perhaps this seems obvious to some, but I had to learn that. And mike is my teacher still. There is so much more to learn from mike. I'm so exhilarated with what I have learned so far and the glories to come. Mike reframed my belief that therapy has to be hard work and suffering, that it has to dredge the bottom of my being, that I have to plow through my muck, over and over, to get healthy. There is some value in looking backwards. I've spent decades doing that. At times, old issues do re-enter my brain. Yes, sometimes they are problematic for me, but mike has awakened in me to live in the now, to experience life in the present, to venture into all those things that are outside myself, and to relish the journey inwards as well. What a dynamic opportunity. Another message from mike is to remove my blinders that only show me what is in front of me, thereby impeding my side views. Since knowing mike, I want to see it all, all the vistas out there that make life worth living. Mike has made me feel renewed, and I'm finding delight in our connection. How wonderful then it is to share this with others. Mike is instrumental in helping me make changes in my life. How can I thank him enough for these treasures? What words would be good enough? What terminology is there to express my joy and jubilation for today? I'm so grateful beyond words. My growth has come about by knowing mike. Through mike's openness and sharing his soul, I found mine. His invitations I couldn't refuse. His willingness to be transparent, how could I not be then, too?

Mike embodies savoring life. He takes time to understand his thoughts and feelings. He relishes in them. When I give him gifts, he doesn't rip off the paper and say, "Thanks." He is involved in the moment. He takes it all in. He is a connoisseur of life, enjoying every morsel with glee and mirth. There are times I am angry with him. He took that in stride also and my reward—I learned I could be angry. I wasn't going to fall apart. I learned when I express my anger towards him, his reaction assures me. He isn't going to strike out at me. I learned that anger isn't a bad bedfellow. It's just one of the human emotions from which we can draw. There is no ranking on feelings. One feeling is not better than another feeling. There are no good or bad feelings. We do have to assume responsibility on how we act on them, how we express them. Mike is comfortable returning my calls, which is important to me. Hearing his voice on the phone gives me extra support between sessions. I never felt there was something wrong with me for having to call him. I needed to call him. He gives me the same message in our sessions. He helps me realize that I'm not just a diagnosis. He reveals his faith in me. Mike being who he is shows me everyone has an inner core, and it is accessible. We all have pools of living waters from which we can draw. If we do, we will thirst no more.

One time, mike had a lapse of judgment, and even in that incident, I learned a valuable lesson. Therapists are like their clients—they aren't perfect either. What a relief that is, but there is no mistake about mike. He transports me into an exciting, virgin world. A world so full of possibilities and fun. One I want to explore along with mike as my guide.

These ideas I wouldn't have understood if I hadn't decided to take that risk, to be engaged with mike. Mike encouraged me to use written words, to express my inner thoughts and feelings. I've been writing letters since then (some good, some not so good). I'm walking with mike on paths leading to new adventures. He extends an invitation that is irresistible. Mike doesn't hide behind a wall of professionalism. He is that, too, but I know him as a fellow traveler. I see him when he is touched. I see him as he thinks. I see him as he feels. I see him as a teacher. I see him mulling. I see his caring. I see his soul. How could I not want to hook up with this ray of hope? He is the lantern who shows me how to go through the dark and how to use my courage to walk back out on the other side of darkness to brightness. Oh, what sweet nectar I deeply swallow from mike's well! Mike teaches me that any of my feelings—angry, sad, dejected, joyful, enthusiastic, euphoric—don't have to engulf me, that I wouldn't lose control, that I'm rational and have emotions, to discover I'm a whole person. I'm unified. I'm not a piece of mind or a piece of feelings. I'm integrated. With mike's assistance, we are still working to diminish my black/white thinking. Mike teaches me there is no "end time" in therapy, that therapy is a living entity. The adventure, on winding roads, doesn't stop as I leave mike's office. Life is never done till it's done, but it's what is in the middle of here and there that matters.

One of the most fantastic things about mike—he gives hugs. I'm enriched by mike's hugs. They give me an even deeper connection with him. I'm in anticipation of many more to come. He tells me those hugs are limitless. The truth is, if mike hadn't come into my life, I wouldn't be rejoicing now. Where is that special word to say how grateful I am for you, mike? There are so many more gifts mike has to share with me. Mike gives me immeasurable presents, and I know there will be more to come. How did I get so lucky?

this letter is my thank-offering for you and for your benevolent grace,

grace

Blast! Blast! Blast! on my radar screen

to three known cherubim—

I made a joyful noise to the Lord for sending my way rebekkah, paul, and mark. Sometimes my darling angels were anything but. They could be little monsters. This reality was more problematic for me since I was expecting "Beech-Nut" babies or at least "Gerber" babies. They came into this world with a mission to educate me as to what's really real about infants. (A little role reversal.) They did a very good job. However, there still was a piece of disappointment for me. To see them as little human beings took getting used to. Before I actually had children, I was swept away with a fantasy – a romantic, sentimental, emotional idealism – seeing infants as make-believe dolls to play with. Why didn't you tell me the truth, mom?

I never understood why sex ed is taught in our public schools. It's actually part of the curriculum. The only way a student can opt out is if his parents refuse to have him participate. Now will someone explain to me why parenting skills aren't taught, as well? Most anyone who wants to can have sex, but none of us have any clue as how to be great parents. It isn't part of curriculums. If we think about it, it is the utmost, positively ultimate, greatest job in all of human history. Sadly, we learn as we go. It becomes an on-the-job training, but we can't hand in our resignations if we don't like the job duties. We may fail learning the skills at our places of employment. We will never be fired as a parent. It's forever even if we are lousy at it. So tell me, why aren't kids being taught how to deal with the possible outcome of having sex? If we have no other information, I've heard from someplace, we tend to parent as our parents parented us. This may or may not be a very good practice. For me, this is a frightening idea. I don't know about you, but I had atrocious parents. They were stinky at it. Regrettably, my kids suffered. I repeated all the mistakes of the past over and over again.

My first munchkin was rebekkah. She always had to do things her own way. She decided to come into her new world "ass-backwards." Only problem with her choice—she didn't get to see the miracle of her journey down the birthing tube. Don't tell me babies being born don't see their process. How do we know for sure they don't? Rebekkah had a special task of proving my ob-gyn doc.'s statements wrong. He told me rebekkah being my first and the fact that she would be a breech presentation, I had plenty of time to get to the hospital. From start to finish, the whole affair took under two hours for her to be in my presence. Rebekkah surely made my labor and delivery a piece of cake. Thanks rebekkah! She came home to a perfect nursery with an imperfect, scared mother. Rebekkah was born with the genes for determination, imagination, intelligence, curiosity, exploration, and living life on her own terms. She was a small person with a big attitude. She just did, acted, without worrying about the consequences. But, this is consistent with being a kid. Her free spirit increased when her brothers were born. She knew I was rather distracted and preoccupied taking care of mark and paul. One bright day, her dad and I couldn't find her. We franticly searched in adjoining yards, then the neighborhood, without finding our little adventurer. We decided to check out the house of one of her playmates. To our despair, we didn't find her. We did find one of rebekkah's sneakers on the sidewalk. Desperation set in. Where could she be? It goes without saying we parents would think and feel the same if we realized we had lost a child, not to know where. With fear mixed with relief, we found rebekkah riding her red tricycle, with one sneaker on, wending her way to the next town to buy gum (she had no $$). This town is about 20 minutes away by car. How could we be angry with her? She had no sense of her actions. Going to buy gum on her bike made sense to her. How would she know her trek wasn't safe? She was so matter-of-fact about her destination and her purpose.

Kids can do very alarming things from their innocence. They see the world as one big jungle gym, they say, "Why don't you get it, mom and dad? My world is so full of things to experience, to understand, to see, to do, to feel, to think about, to find, to have gusto, to find joy, and have fun doing it. Try to understand how the world seems to us kids;

can you join us there? Can you remember being our size? Can you recapture the magic of it all? Why do you threaten us when we do something you don't like instead of explaining a better way to behave? Even with all the responsibilities of being grown up we little kids know that, if you look hard enough, you will find your own child is still there waiting to be rediscovered. We only ask you to keep us safe.

Do you know any 2 ½-year-old kid who had the opportunity to be kicked by a horse and propelled across the barnyard, with only bruises to attest to the incident? Say hello, to my rebekkah. Another day, on coming home from church, I got out of the car and turned my back briefly while the kids were still in the car. As I turned, I realized rebekkah had figured out what that stick was near the steering wheel. In horror, I watched rebekkah in the driver's seat, and mark and paul in the back seat, slowly backing down the driveway. Rebekkah's escapades certainly taught me how to be more observant and more aware of possible disasters before they happen, especially around her. And remember, she was only a toddler—oh what was to come as she grew? (Do you think she will survive childhood?) I also believed her other purpose here on earth was to keep me from getting bored. That was impossible as she dazzled everything around her. She was quite visible and verbal, which made her a sparkling star and there was no taking her for granted. She let her actions follow her heart's voice. How else would I have all my treasured memories of her distinctive style, her being a free thinker? To my firstborn—praises.

Munchkins 2 and 3 arrived. Rebekkah, her father, and I had the biggest shock of our lives. Since it was too crowded in the womb, paul and mark came early into their new family. The only problem with that was mark and paul forgot to tell us there would be two of them, looking exactly alike. The docs. didn't know either. In my day, there was no invention called "amniocentesis." I'm sure you are saying, "Good grief—how primitive!" The idea of having twins was too hard for me to grasp. I went into a panic mode. Our nursery was only set up for the one child we thought was to join us at our home. Mark and paul were born preemies, so they stayed extra time in the hospital, affording us time to scramble together all the baby things we needed for our second son. To ensure no nighttime interruptions for dave, and rebekkah; paul, mark, and I set up camp at the far end of our living room. The boys slept in porta cribs; I slept in a twin bed beside them. I use the word "slept" rather loosely. I didn't sleep very much at all. With this arrangement that lasted over six months, I was relegated to care for the twins all by myself. I was beyond exhaustion, and so overwhelmed. I asked myself a lot, "Can I keep doing this?" Being premature, they ate every two hours or so. Even in the beginning, when one twin cried to be fed, I would wake the other to feed them both at the same time, whether he was hungry or not. I treated them the same. My intended belief was to recognize mark and paul as separate kids, each having his own identity. My behaviors contradicted that view. I lumped the guys' needs together. They had to have told themselves, "Don't listen to what our own bodies tell us. I'm not hungry, but my mother is waking me up to feed me. I really want to sleep." I wonder sometimes how all this parenting may have affected mark and paul's sense of being able to get their own needs met in the here and now, rather than having someone outside themselves deciding for them. Paul and mark, like rebekkah, were curious, explorative, bright, creative, and imaginative. The difference was these qualities were multiplied by two. There is a saying about twins—"Double trouble." I wondered if that was true. But I was too busy to think about it. Okay, which determined kid do I try to catch first as both crawl away in different directions? Having to make this decision all day long was quite a challenge. I wish I could have been an octopus.

At the start, I used their hospital bands to tell the little guys apart. When they outgrew them, I painted nail polish on the toenail and fingernail of mark, or was it paul? The good news – paul and mark eventually came to know who they were. They weren't so lucky with others knowing them as two boys, not one boy, especially with their schoolmates. They were either not called their name at all or when they ran cross country or participated in track events, everyone cheered them on by yelling out, "Go, Cote. Go, Cote." On many levels, mark and paul's existence was experienced as attached at the hip. Others treated mark and paul as I did when they were babies—they both had to eat and sleep at the same time—not perceived as individuals. Most people think twins are so unusual, so sweet. They like having double vision, I guess. Rebekkah got lost in all of this drama. I would push the boys in their carriage with rebekkah walking beside me. People we met would "oh" and "ah" over the twins, with no words or recognition for rebekkah. You know that had to hurt. Rebekkah loved to be read to. It was one of her favorite activities. With all this reading to her, plus watching *Sesame Street* and *The Electric Company* on TV, rebekkah learned to read all by herself long before she entered kindergarten. You might be asking, "What is that last show? I've never heard of it." Let me tell you—it was a successful program in the late 60s that was geared to help kids start the reading process with pizzazz. It was electrifying.

After the boys were born, when I would start to read bedtime stories to her, I would fall asleep instead of her.

I never dressed the twins alike, but it was easier to keep them the same in other ways. Everything had to be "fair" for each of them. If one kid made Little League and not the other, then neither of them could be on the team. Now is this convoluted thinking or not? I'm the one who was "unfair" to both of them. From my experiences with paul and mark, being a twin has a lot of flaws. It's not always cute. What each had to do to struggle to emerge as his own person took a lot of courage, and I and others didn't always help them accomplish this when we found it more expedient to see them as one. It suited our needs. It made our lives easier to connect with mark and paul without knowing their names. It also took rebekkah a lot of courage to find her way when people only saw her "cute" twins. How shameful!

As soon as the kids were born into our family, they were given a label—PKs. They were not only labeled, they were also heaped with tons of expectations from others. It might be difficult for you to fathom how troublesome this might be for a youngster. Their set roles were even harder to achieve because the expectations for their behaviors came from all fronts. They needed to be perfect. The messages came from the community, the school, and especially church members. This seemed to be a burden my kids shouldn't have had to bear. It was hard enough for me to be a pastor's wife, but I chose to marry a man who became a pastor. Granted, I was naïve about that too, but I was not a kid who had no options. Their dad decided in what church involvements they were going to participate, which was most. He never asked them. Then I came along with a double whammy. I colluded with dave. I tried to please dave and members of the church at the same time. Guess who got lost in this loony predicament? I denied my own kids their right to be who they were, to be unconditionally loved as the special, unique, awesome kids they were (and still are). Rebekkah, paul, and mark certainly had additional challenges to overcome, and I'm taking a risk here to say they had more to deal with in the self-discovery process than most other kids. They had to take oppressive, warped feedback from their surroundings, redefine it, reprocess it, and re-inherit their beautiful souls. They did it! Let me tell you, they are still evolving into ever-changing, marvelous persons. I celebrate you, rebekkah, my daughter, my darling! I celebrate you, paul, my son, my darling! I celebrate you, mark, my son, my darling! My kids shared themselves with me, which caused my life to be extraordinary. Now you may understand why I used the salutation I did for this letter. Rebekkah, mark, and paul were my precious cherubim! (They still are.)

After reading about this time in my life with my kids, you can see why I have so many regrets and why I still grieve. That time in history can never be redone. The kids' childhood is past; scars may linger from my mothering skills, or lack thereof, back then. I can't travel in reverse to fix them. Sad to report, I didn't get my life together until the kids graduated from college. Try to imagine how many years of my life with my kids were lost—my not sharing, loving, giving, or supporting them. I lost not having loving bonds with them. I felt all those things, but I lived by a code that what others thought about dave, rebekkah, mark, paul, and me was my primary duty to strive for. I'm sure you figured out the theme of our early years as a family. Deny your individuality and sacrifice who you are in order to meet others' expectations. God has granted me time to change my unhealthy relationship from the past with rebekkah, paul, and mark. I'm profoundly grateful for His gift! Can you believe my kids say, "I love you"? They have forgiven my mistakes, have shared their compassion, and have given me their greatest present—acknowledgement that we are not to be lumped together; we are not defined by others; we each have our own spirit, essence, inner self to explore, then to be able to share this with other minds and souls. How did I get so lucky to have rebekkah, paul, and mark in my life? I'm forever grateful!

Parenting being the most daunting job there is, let's make it work. It's a full-time occupation. It never ends. There is always room for improvement if we seek it. Don't wait till your kids graduate from college, like I did, to have a right relationship with them. Carrying around my guilt for my past mothering is a huge, heavy load. It feels awful. Realizing my kids didn't have a mother they deserved still feels bad. Believe me, you don't want to carry a bale like mine. Remember, cherish those little people who are entrusted to our care. Take the time. What blessings they are! If we let them, they have a lot to teach us, too. With zest, let's be a fantastic parent! This is the greatest venture in all of our lives—there is no other. Our actions will affect kids for generations to come. The universe cares.

from one caretaker to another, hallowed be us parents

would a lobotomy help?

to a known black or white brain—

While being with my soulful presence, he became my "creative consultant" again. He knows I have been struggling most of my life to turn around my black or white thinking. It's such a part of me. I rarely know I'm being caught up in it. Perhaps this letter could be therapeutic.

Then on the way home, I got to thinking, "What's wrong with black or white living?" I noticed there was black asphalt divided by white lines. All the signs along the highway were white with black letters. They said which highway the driver was on and other pertinent information. Some people buy either black or white autos. They cost less than colored cars. In the 60s, women wanted to wear black and white checkered suits. (Jackie Kennedy was the first to wear one.) There is salt and pepper. Herringbone sports jackets are popular in men's wear. In my day, photos only came in black and white. Our tiny TV set only came in black and white. One of my favorite drinks at the soda fountain was a black and white soda (it had chocolate syrup, vanilla ice cream and seltzer water, topped with mounds and mounds of whipped cream). Then there are all those nametags with black background and white letters. I've even seen black and white floor tiles, making a checkered pattern. I know for sure you have seen referees running around in their black and white uniforms. And the utmost in formal wear is the black and white tuxedo.

These things are in my world. I ask again, "What's wrong with black or white thinking?" We live in a society of: on/off; here/there; fast/slow; high/low; inside/outside; all/nothing; life/death; night/day; forward/backward; blessings/woes; upper/lower; love/hate; etc, etc, in a good or bad world. I think you get my point. The whole world functions with opposites. That way, the meaning of words is established and very clear. We don't have to be concerned that we might be confusing in our conversations with others. So, again, why do I need to change these common practices, the norm? Why should I be any different? Aren't I like most people?

Well, I had a bunch of clinicians who wanted to change my black or white thinking. They wanted me to see the light instead of the dark. What do I know? The therapists were smarter than me. What do I know? I'm only the patient. There were some who gave their best shot. I admired all their book knowledge. There were testimonies to that fact by all their degrees hanging on the walls. There were framed documents attesting to their advanced training and to the associations to which they belonged: APA; MAPA; MSW; MSW, LSW; MED; MSW, LLL; MS; LCP, NCC; MD; PhD; PAPA. They worked in private practice. They worked in clinics. They worked in hospitals. They could provide counseling services for children and adolescents, marriage counseling, group therapy, geriatric counseling, individual counseling, relationship counseling, essence of life counseling, safety network counseling, susquehanna house of courage counseling, interconnections counseling, spiritual counseling, or good hope counseling (how misinformed—of course hope is good.), etc. etc. etc. We certainly have a lot of choices. I'm positive they want to change us. It's their job. With all these facilitators, how come I still see everything around me in black or white? Is it because I didn't try hard enough? Maybe it was because I was too resistant to both the therapy and the therapist? Counselors tend to use this term when we don't make progress in treatment. How can they expect us to grow and change when it's our fault when it doesn't happen? We have all these distressing symptoms, and we seek help. And then you blame us when you can't help us. Oh yes, of course, we are the clients. It makes sense. We haven't a clue about what's going on within ourselves. Only you know what has to be fixed in us. You have the power to accomplish that goal. "Why aren't I getting better?", "How many years will it take for me to get better?" "You gotta be kidding. Now, I'm in a rock and a hard place."

I don't know what all the fuss is about. Actually, I like the way I am. Viewing the world in black or white is very comfortable, secure, and familiar. What fouled it up was those people with the credentials gave me a diagnosis. Then they really worked harder to cure me. Now it is official—I'm 301.83, or at least that's what the DSM-IV said. Really, I don't have to think as much when I divide the world into either/ors. It gets confusing to me when I have to think of alternatives. I pride myself in making quick decisions. It's front or back. People who weigh all the options scare me. How will they know if they are right or wrong? It could be a wrong answer, and as for me, I'll go ballistic. I can't focus on this anymore. I have a more important disorder. Now I'm 296.5x as well as 301.83. It's about mood swings. I feel either high or low. The doc. wants to prescribe Rx's. By doing so, I would be stabilized, but being in the middle is no fun. There definitely is more excitement feeling like a yo-yo. Is it possible to be maintained with Rx's? Can I imagine seeing the world in chromatic brilliance? Can I work on my black or white thinking? I realize all those therapists from the past couldn't fix me if I didn't want to be. I have to want to deal with my black and white traits. I'll tell you, that's a tall order. Black or white thinking is so entrenched. A lot of times I don't even know I'm doing it. It will be hard to identify. To be aware of my process, I will need to understand how my fixated head works. Do I really want to let go of my simple view of the world? Are choices really necessary?

I come by my black or white processing legit. It was passed down from my gene pool. My folks were good role models for the condition. We kids have the DNA for black or white thinking. I'm stuck in extremes. My mentality is based on polarizations. I distort feedback from others. In my mind, whatever others say or do, I believe they are saying either I did a good job or I didn't. If I believe others are saying I did a poor job, I get very angry at them. Either I'm perfect or I'm a S.O.B. I haven't been able to settle into gray areas or into the middles. What makes my black or white thinking difficult is I judge my own worth on what's going on in my brain, not the facts. I have my own internal barometer that filters what I hear or see around me. I have a hard time accepting that some things can't be measured in my black or white world. I take offense very easily. By twisting in my head what I think you are suggesting, I will lash out at you, and you won't have a clue as to what's going on. You won't understand my anger. This internal battle to always be on top, be successful all the time, hurts. My need to strive for perfection. How hard it would be to see my world in gradations. As a kaleidoscope of colors. It would be wonderful if I could control my black or white thinking. The pressure to be always right, and if not, I'm wrong, has given me a permanent tension headache. I overreact to stimuli from my mindset. I take in information to determine if I'm up or down, but I can't tolerate being in the down position. Is there really a place between black or white? It's scary to think about. If I'm in the middle, how do I act? What am I supposed to be? How can I stop sabotaging myself? How can I teach myself a new language? How can I accept that I do some things okay and other things so-so? How to get the weight of expectations off my back? How to stop condemning myself for not being perfect? How to stop thinking others are condemning me?

Don't you dare say this letter could use more work. It has to be superb, or I'm a failure. I have fears about change. I'm in a strange and unknown world, and I don't have a guide dog. Can I walk around my wall of absolutes? Doing so could grant me some peace. I wouldn't have to continually strive for first place. I could stop judging myself for not being the best all the time. I could stop assuming others are putting me into black or white positions. Accept that others don't function in my orbit. To stop assuming others are evaluating me from my frame of reference. That others don't think in black or white terms as I do. To stop believing others are judging me when I'm the one processing reality through distorted glasses. It could be less difficult if I eliminated the absolute categories in my brain. How less difficult it could be for me if I stop assuming others have the same perceptions as I do. Others' feedback is not really an attempt to put me at the bottom of the heap, nor is it necessary to think the other spot is at the top. I ask myself, "Do I have the courage and stamina to work on these dynamics?"

No wiz kid of a therapist could have made me stop my black or white thinking. As in any therapeutic relationship, there is need for support, the kind of support that enables us to face our ghostly, cobwebbed, shrieking messages going around in our heads. Am I willing to work with my soulful presence as a team, while not abdicating my power to work on changing myself, for my best helper is me? And I'm going to help me by making a decision to do just that. I'm the only one who can discard my black or white thinking and replace it with a rainbow hue. It seems to me there are many questions in this letter for me to answer. As in AA, I'm doing the steps toward recovery from my addiction to black or white thinking.

if you, "unknown readers," don't think this letter is spectacular,
I promise I won't feel deficient

to an unknown writer—

After a successful interview, my soulful presence, mike, got the job. His new title is "creative consultant." The salary he gets isn't near what he's worth nor does he get any life assurances. The last time we were talking, he came up with the idea of writing a letter to the salutation above. What did he mean by that suggestion? Should I write about my writing process or me? Umh! It's a given; I'm unknown to you.

I have to admit, I do have a love affair with my trusty, cheap pen. It is a white one with a black top. There are words on its side. It says, "Bic, round stic, med/moy." How about that? They can't even spell "stick" right. *And what does all the other gobbly gook mean?* you're asking. I don't have a clue, but at least it works for awhile. My biggest passion though is my yellow, legal-sized with blue lines sheets of paper.

One of the things I do is write billions, trillions x trillions x trillions of words. Do you happen to know what the highest measuring number could be? The highest I can go is a trillion. I was lousy in math. So I will just say the numbers are incomprehensible. I write into the early morning hours, but I get a wonderful gift. I get to see when the first light has its birth, but like a lot of things, there is the down side, too. I wake up feeling groggy because I was fighting six-winged seraphims and cherubims who were turquoise all night. Or was I fighting the Wicked Witch of the West with her stupid, monotonous, obnoxious, brown, flying monkeys all night? There are times when I'm fighting chartreuse sea monsters. Or fiery red beasties of prey. My other sleep problem is so many words; sentences are ravaging my brain with no respect that I'm getting sleep deprived. When all these words and ideas come, I'm compelled to jump out of bed and rush to my dining room, where I write them down on my yellow, legal-sized with blue lines sheets of paper so I won't forget them. Yeah, I know, you are wondering why I don't have a yellow, legal-sized with blue lines pad next to my bed? Duh, dingbat, why didn't I think of that? At least I'm not hearing voices, unless they are singing, or seeing things that aren't there, unless I'm seeing the faces of my kids. Do you think there is a Rx to take care of a "racing thoughts syndrome"? I don't think so. I haven't seen any advertised on my TV, but there is a lot of snake oil being peddled. (Listen carefully to those hastily mentioned side effects.)

I don't think you really care if I only use two fingers to type. I don't think you really care if I don't look at the screen, although sometimes those wavy red lines catch my attention. I make bushels of mistakes, so the editing is a pain in the a**. My thoughts flow like a bubbling brook, making delightful sounds, skipping over things in their path. It's almost magical, like it's out of my control. There is a phrase, "It's a labor of love." Not for me. I groove on the "love" part. What I do, I love. Sometimes I think I have diarrhea of thoughts, though, but I'm not willing to take Imodium, or even Imodium Advanced, for my condition. How to fix this problem, I say? Solution: I take all my words, thoughts I have written down on, you can fill in the blanks…I pick all of them up from my dining room floor and put them into file folders, which are a drab, sickly color. (Do you think some iron pills might help?) There are oodles of writings, for I write more words than I need for one letter, but I save what is left over on my yellow, legal-size with blue lines sheets of paper. I can always use them for another day.

By now, you must be completely, totally bored. If my soulful presence meant to write about my process of writing my letters, what difference does it make to you? Who cares? Like, who cares what ingredients are in a gourmet meal? Only if it's an experience to die for. (We don't mean that.) Do we use other words that have nothing to do with their real meanings? It can be confusing if we use slang all the time in our conversations with others—unless we can find a slang dictionary. Oh, sorry, sometimes I get off track. Getting back to that meal, who wants to know the process to make the meal? We only care about the finished product, right? A finished product we can develop, market, sell, and make lots of $$.

If my soulful presence meant to write about the writer, me, I don't think you would care about that either. Do you really care I have no allergies? Do you really care what my major or minor were in college umpteen years ago? (Luckily, I've learned a whole lot more about living since then.) Do you really care about all the surgeries? Do you really care that once in a while I need to see a cardiologist to fix my sad, broken-down heart? Symptoms I have once in a while. I wonder why now they call broken hearts "cardiac arrests"? Whatever happened to the good old heart attack? Do we need to be so clinical? So uppity? Or is it the medical profession who wants to use words we aren't quite sure what they mean? "You really need to give me simple explanations instead of doctorize, doc." Do you really care I wear a phony look-alike linen jacket to church? Do you really care I graduated from grad school? That sounds redundant. (Just another piece of paper to file away.) Do you really care that I want to go back to live in New England? I so miss that ocean. An awesome creation of God. Do you really want to know the color of the ocean up there? It's a sorta blue, mixed with a sorta brown, unless the "red tide" comes rolling in—then it's red. I bet that took you by surprise. (That means no swimming—boo!) Even the seaweed is a disgusting color, but it is a timeless beauty, and I sure miss it. Wouldn't it be great for landlocked folks to be able to print the ocean out on our Brothers HL 2020 laser printer? Sad to say, we can't type the ocean into our Microsoft Word documents either, and it's the pits we can't go online either, not even on e-bay. Do you really care that by writing personal letters I can break a lot of the rules? (You know, all those rules somebody else makes up for us.) Whee! I'm having so much fun creating my own rules. Do you really care what the size of my underwear is? Or what kind? Is it those thongs? Oh, witless one, those are flip-flops. Do you really give a rip about any of this stuff? By now, you must be ready to take that tried and true remote control to change channels. You could push the delete button and hold it down for a long while. Is all of this rambling becoming a drag for you? Are you saying, "Finish it, please?"

Perchance (a $.25 cent word), there is something in this letter that might have some relevancy to you, the reader. I says to myself, you might be interested to know I feel very humbled sharing my words with you. If I do have a gift to write stuff, I take no credit for it. If I have a gift, it would have come from God. His gift graciously sent my way. I constantly wonder if what I write (on yellow, legal-size with blue lines sheets of paper) has some meaning to you, my "unknown readers." It has been more than an exciting and fulfilling endeavor for me. I have gotten reams and reams of yellow, legal-size with blue lines sheets of paper from my venture. I'm jubilant! By putting down all the words in my letters, that I share with you, readers, causes me to feel triumphant.

But none of the facts of my writing style or the details of me have anything to do with the "unknown writer." For, you see, the letters are me. I'm the letters. If you chose to read my letters, you might come to know something more about the "unknown writer." The secret about how I write is I take the ordinary and try to make it into something extraordinary. Gee, maybe I should apply for a patent for my secret? I sure don't want anyone else to steal my secret, but when all is said and done, the truth of the matter is everyone has to find his or her own secret.

Whatta you say?

am I little less of "an unknown writer"?

to an all too familiar body—

If we were created in God's image, why aren't our bodies perfect? Maybe there is perfection in the body politic. Or perhaps it is found in the body of believers. Is there perfection in our body's guards? Certainly body bags are no fun. I know that anatomy 107 1/2 teaches perfection. All those pictures and diagrams portray our bodies as all being alike, but my vertebra is shot. Is yours? And what the hell is a cranial cavity? Do wisdom teeth really make us wise? That's a silly question. Most of us have them removed long before we are wise. I'm sure our brain stems are working. What's this right brain/left brain thing all about? I didn't know I have a descending colon, a transverse colon, and an ascending colon. Did you? Oh, there goes my viscera acting up again. Forget my abs. I'll tell you, one thing your body doesn't want to be is a corpse.

We all feel hunger. Our taste buds are perfectly fine tuned. Each of us has our favorite food repertoire. And some people, like me, put too much of that favorite food on our plates. I'm a dessert person. When I go out to eat, I always look at the dessert menu first. The main menu is so humdrum. Really, how many ways can you prepare chicken? It still tastes like chicken. I figure why should I spend good money for a different sauce on my chicken when I can make it at home? Oh, but those desserts are works of art. I would never order brownies with vanilla ice cream and chocolate sauce either. I can make that at home, too. If desserts weren't the most important items to order, why would they be called "happy endings"? Don't be fooled. It's not mother's milk that comforts us—it's chocolate. Can I sell you my spare tire? I have plenty to spare. At least I have a skinny skeleton. Why do you think God built us so we can put on weight so easily? Maybe He is trying to show us how funny He is, because taking the weight off is a bitch. And that's not funny! Even though the stomach that is fed too much can cause millions of diseases and be life threatening, it doesn't scare us.

Rest assured, we do have a funny bone to help us laugh, but then we have that nervous system which makes us fidgety and anxious. And where is the soul located in our bodies? Can it be surgically removed to make it more caring. Is this more helpful? In what part of the cardio-vascular system does love reign? With all my education, I haven't found the place in our bodies that holds the human spirit. I'm still trying to select what color button I want sewn into my belly. Did you know that docs. blow up balloons and put them into coronary arteries? The bummer—they don't invite the rest of us to the party. They don't even serve cake and ice cream either—just those stupid balloons.

Did you now there is a doc. for every part of our bodies? They call themselves "specialists." I think that means they have to be in med school longer. You certainly don't want to go to a pulmonary guy when you really need to see an ophthalmologist. You won't get your eyes fixed if you go to a lung doc. (Can you tell me why most docs' titles all end in "ists"?) I think you get the picture. We really do come in pieces, even though we came into the office as a whole body. A psychiatrist once told me the brain is part of the body, so there is no such thing as mental illness. It's a body illness. That was good to know, but can you tell me where the "me" is in my brain?

My soulful presence and I are working on my "body image" problem. Needless to say, going to the root of my problems with bodies brings me back to mom and dad. Of course, I know I can't blame *everything* on them, but I'm going to try. My parents skipped a generation or two. They went from Victorian to Victorian (without the secret). They denied I even had a body. At least I didn't have to wear a berka. It was okay to show my face. My folks did the same as those doc. specialists do, only I was broken into a good or bad body part. I became a head with two arms walking around on two legs. What's in between, the torso, doesn't exist, especially genitalia. To accomplish this reality, I hide my body with loose-fitting clothes. I never wear shorts to any official, professional offices. I might wear shorts to the mall because there I blend in with the crowd. I'm not a person. Capri pants work. When

I wear sandals, I wear ankle socks so no one can see my feet. Feet are ugly, too. Can't show too much skin, you know. I haven't worn a bathing suit in centuries. And now that I'm old, I work very hard to cover every bulge, saggy part, roll of fat, and hanging flesh I can. Unfortunately, my crinkly alligator skin is impossible to hide. Not to mention all those wrinkles that show. Yeah, I know, there are magical creams I can buy to make my wrinkles vanish. To get rid of my wrinkles, only a jackhammer will do.

A body that has been violated on many levels for a long time goes numb. That body decides it is shameful and dirty. Guilt abounds. This bruised body never felt a loving touch. It was never hugged. It never heard words of encouragement for its emerging feminine body. This body was never told being a woman was a joy to be savored. It was never told the human body is elegant. This body was never told it was all right to accept itself. This body learned that intimacy hurts. This body was confused a lot. It could never understand why it was being assaulted. This body doesn't seek pleasure. This body wondered if other little bodies endured this kind of pain. This body is unable to love other bodies. This body just wanted to feel safe. This body shuts down when other bodies come too close. This body was angry at God. Locked inside this body was rage. This body tried to destroy itself. This body longed for another body to come and help it. It wanted another body to be there for it. This body doesn't want to feel helpless and hopeless anymore. This body doesn't want to feel like a victim anymore. This body wants to find peace in itself.

with love,
"the unknown writer"

to 3 sort a known childhoods—

Say hello to my sisters: Reinholdine, affectionately known as reiny, and Deborah, affectionately known as debbie. I was called wannie. Reiny is my middle sister, and that being said, obviously debbie is the youngest. Ohm! Where to start this letter? Sisters just are. Who thinks about it? What is sisterhood all about? What's being a "family" all about anyway? Hello, who are we? I know we are sisters, but who are we? I know it isn't all about those sweet messages found in a Hallmark card. (Sorry to disappoint you.) In our family, we weren't individuals. That was against house policy, as well as all the other rules we kids had to follow. (Believe me, they were not "child friendly.") My only concern about writing this letter—I might offend my sisters. Their recollections might be different. I might make mistakes in the accuracy of the details. Reiny and deb, please remember this letter is only from my point of view. It is filtered through my contact lenses. (But I don't wear contacts.)

Now that I have decided to go ahead and write about growing up with my two sisters, I'm bummed! I'm blank. I can't remember much. I don't have many memories of that time in our lives together. I guess we can't remember all the facts of our day-to-day living. I guess our brains would be too full of the mundane. We have more important data to store away. Is it easier to robotically walk through our lives? My life may not pertain to your experiences, but I hope you will read on. And yet, why can't I find the most important part of all our relationships? I can recall a special meal. The most notable—a fancy French dish consisting of opened, black-shelled mussels in red sauce, which was delightfully served to us kids. Do I have to tell you what our reactions were? You see, the three of us weren't into gourmet yet. Yuck! What were you thinking, mom? Needless to say, the three of us went without supper and to bed hungry. (Unfortunately, this happened a lot.) I can recall our house (except my bedroom). I can see my back yard. Although in trying to write this letter, I ask, "What was my connection with reiny and debbie?" The reason given for our not being close was due to our age differences. Reiny is five years younger then I, and debbie is almost a decade. I don't buy that rationale any longer. It wasn't the truth. Come to think of it, the three of us lived with distortions of reality, not truths.

In the turmoiled, oppressive, deadly, violent atmosphere within our family, each of us chose our own way to cope and survive. Reiny became the rebellious child. She went out of her way to defy "the rules." The down side to her stance—she got hit a whole lot. Even when she tried to be helpful by bringing in the milk bottles (back then milk was actually left at your doorstep by a milkman). Crossing through the dining room, she dropped one of the bottles, spilling milk all over the rug. Dad went into his usual angry rage, striking her across the face, sending her glasses flying, her face to bleed. The constant message: we can't make mistakes; accidents are unacceptable; we need to understand that things, carpets, are more important than us. Can you imagine what trying to be perfect is like? We needed to keep safe from the devouring lion father. And mom never protected us. She stood by and did nothing. The three of us were on our own. Reiny, can't you follow the rules, get with the program? Can't you behave? No matter how crazy the system we lived in, is standing up for your individuality worth it? You know, reiny, constantly seeing you physically assaulted was hard for debbie and I to witness. We were helpless in trying to save you from it. I took from these scenes the lessons that I have no control over myself or my environment. I'm a victim. There is no salvation. I'm sure there are many of you who have experienced similar childhoods. I was thinking maybe there should be an entrance exam before one can be entrusted with raising children, to be able to enter parenthood. But there may be some would-be parents who would cheat, not so much to get kids, but only to compete with the other participants for the highest score on the test.

About the only thing I had in common with debbie was our shared coping mechanisms. (You need to know when she went to kindergarten, I was already in high school.) I knew debbie, but I didn't know her. She was my baby sister, with the emphasis on *baby*. Besides this fact, debbie also decided to lay low, under the radar, to survive. So even when debbie and I were in the now, our real selves were shrouded. Escaping from the conflict and insane dynamics of living in our house was a good idea for reiny, debbie, and me. Reiny escaped the scene by riding her bike all over town till dusk. Certainly you can guess she knew the lay of the land. Only problem—I didn't know what they were all about, and they didn't know about me, either, which was okay because I didn't know me anyway. Our disguises worked. We didn't take off our masks, even when Halloween was over. Sadly, our choices for self-preservation separated us from one another. We were isolated in our own pain. So alone. How can we find ourselves in a home where it is forbidden to do that? Being depersonalized kinda thwarts budding of self. Even to the detriment of our health, it is hard to let go of all the maladaptive behaviors, thoughts and feelings that have been a challenge for reiny, debbie, and me. I joined reiny and debbie. We found solace in withdrawing, not only in our heads but by escaping the unbearable scenes—to run away. It's too bad for reiny she didn't run away enough. Let's pretend it wasn't happening—deny it. We need to ask, "Who are we? Do we have a clue? Do you know what the word 'identity' means? It's so overwhelming. Where do we start?" It is much easier to hold onto the safe, the old, the familiar, even though it hurts us now. I further annihilated myself by building a New England wall around me. A New England wall consists of stones placed atop each other, both very long and wide—a fortified barrier. There is no adhesive joining each stone. There are no cracks to peer through. If you are behind a wall such as this, you will be hidden. You might be asking yourself, "How sturdy can this wall be?" To answer your question, it was created since mankind hit the New England shores and is still standing. Some rocks may fall to the earth, but the basic wall stays intact. I was secure behind my wall. Why would I want to abandon the safety of my stone fortress? The only way I chanced exposure, leaving my sanctuary, was gained by "helpers" reaching out to hold my hand and leading me to safe havens. There is a Bible verse that says, "If you know the truth, the truth will set you free."

Reiny, debbie and I lived with contradictions. We were confused a lot. On one hand, we existed in our own separate worlds. On the other, we were lumped together—just one entity, not three. Our folks' words and actions weren't the same; they didn't match. Which one should we believe—what you say or what you do? We had to do everything together. Like a well-oiled machine, the sum is greater than the parts. If the engine runs, who cares about the other components under the hood? We kids would rather go play with our friends than join the family brigade to weed the garden. Why is killing weeds better than connections and fun? Of course, you figured out who prevailed. The rules were rigidly set in concrete.

"You can wear lipstick when you are a freshman."

"You can't open an unopened box of cereal until you finish the old one first."

"You can have a record player in the sixth grade."

"Others are out to get you—don't trust anyone."

"Men are sobs" (mom's message.)

"You can't wear red shoes because others would think you're suicidal."

"One drink and you're an alcoholic." (They were obsessed with this topic.)

Our grandmother kept scaring us when she would say, "TV is the agent of the devil."

And what about all those fun things we could have done had our parents not put them on their sinful list? At one point, our parents owned a primitive summer cottage with an outhouse on a small lake in New Jersey. When the summer season ended, we were forced to eat up all the leftover ice cream. You may be saying, "What's so bad about that? I love ice cream." Would you want to eat so much ice cream you got sick and wanted to throw up? To this day, debbie can't eat vanilla/chocolate/strawberry ice cream (my parents' favorite, so we had a lot of it). Can anyone explain to me why consuming all that ice cream was more important than our needs? Do we really have to be punished to save a few pennies? Please see us as little people with our own needs, mom and dad!

Mom was full of threats, criticism, and judgments. Her favorite method to disseminate her opinions and beliefs was by quoting from the Bible—"the good book" as she called it. Her version of the "good book" wasn't very good. The passages, taken out of context, were to tell reiny and I to shape up. None of the verses she selected were to help us come to know a loving God. The bottom line—she used texts that proved how bad reiny and I were in her eyes and God's. When reiny and I fought, mom would take out her "good book" and say, "If you can't love your sister, you can't love God." To be accurate, it is supposed to be brother, not sister, but mom could always make anything fit for her purposes. (Actually, fighting with your siblings is good practice for the adult wars to come.) Well! How can we overcome an un-forgiving, self-righteous, hateful mother and a damning God? We couldn't. Hell, here we come! To compound our badness, one Christmas mom decided to put coal in our stockings (that's all we got). Now it's solidified – mom, God, and now even Santa believed we were as bad as sin, with no hope for redemption! (We didn't have a chance in hell, but that's where we were going anyhow.) Why bother? We were doomed. I wonder what fire and brimstone smells like?

By being the oldest, I had the misfortune of being the pathfinder. What I did well in, what I failed at, became the norm for reiny and debbie. I started taking ballet lessons. (No one asked me if I wanted to.) It became clear to me I had neither the body shape nor the agility to even think about becoming a ballerina. I couldn't even straighten my leg up to the bar. One of the sacred rules: if I failed at ballet, reiny and debbie wouldn't even get a chance at it. We had to get the same grades in the same courses. And even when we did, it was never good enough. I felt a lot of guilt that my failures impacted reiny's and debbie's op-portunities. Another rule to change: We are, in fact, loveable. We aren't accepting the old messages anymore. Reiny, debbie, and I have been given time to get beyond just surviving in order to embrace new life, as we are, who we are.

One bedtime story I read to my kids was *Are You My Mother?* by P.D. Eastman. Isn't it amazing how children's stories make truths sim-ple and understandable? The short of it—while a mother bird goes off to find food for her about-to-be-born baby bird, the baby bird breaks out of his shell and wonders where his mother is. He sets out to find her. Eastman writes, "He couldn't fly, but he could walk." He comes upon a kitten, hen, dog, and cow. They tell him they aren't his mother. Determined, the baby bird continues on. He comes to a big "snort" (a steam shovel). He states, "You aren't my mother. You are a scary snort." Eastman writes, "Then the snort lifted the baby bird up and dropped him back in the tree," back in his nest. The mother bird returned. "I know who you are," said the baby bird. "You are not a kitten, hen, dog, cow, or snort! You are a bird, and you are my mother!" What a mar-velous bond. The baby bird knew his mother; his mother knew him. The baby bird trusted his mother. He knew he would be cared for, loved, and be safe in his nest. Did you have such a bond with a loving, caring mom like the baby bird—a mother you knew, a mother who knew you, and who you trusted? Be grateful if you did. Reiny, debbie and I didn't.

For one of the last pieces for me to explore—and by doing so, I hope to find inner peace and freedom from the past. I had to be willing to unveil a repressed memory: a dirty, heinous, tortured secret. It was so buried it only surfaced in my old age, after years of therapy. In some ways, the secret is still a secret. I haven't talked about it in depth with anyone. My sisters don't even know. In other letters I've shared with you, I honestly and forthrightly divulged myself. I think you have seen my soul behind the words. I fervently hope so! The whole point, what it was all about, was my attempt to connect with your soul. If I did, oh! such bliss. I'm about to entrust you with my excruciating secret. Can you be there with me? I finally came to see the truth, and the truth set me free. Into my awareness came the truth that my mother sexually molested me as a young kid. That truth set me free! I'm free at last! I'm free at last! From a schizophrenic past to the freedom land. Let the healing continue! Pax!

join me in walking the freedom trail

watch for that merge sign

to an unknown motorist—

With this salutation, maybe this time I can interest more "unknown readers." Most everyone drives. I think I'm right on this one.

After being with my soulful presence, the unspeakable happened. It was a tragedy in the making. I was bobbing along on Routes 11/15. I was seeing trees making a huge effort to have their baby yellow-green-ish leaves turn into real adult leaves. They certainly were attracting my senses. It seemed to me the baby leaves were bursting and bursting to give us shade. The babies were striving to create a new, darker-green color, which would last until that amazing Technicolor of fall. The Susquehanna River was on my right, rolling along. Who knows where it was going. I know you map enthusiasts will say, "Well, it is either going N/S/E/W." In my imagination, I'm wondering where that river mind is *really* going. Perhaps it has a blind date with a tributary. (It could, you know.) One thing I never will understand—why every once in a while it decides to flow beyond its limits. I'm thinking, would the Susquehanna River ever reach the magnitude of "That Old Man River?" It might have the distinction of being "That Young Toddler River."

Back to the troubling experience. I was motoring along with my mind on the trees, the river, and all my thoughts. I was putting them in my save bin, in my head's storage compartment. Then in my pe-ripheral vision, there was something I didn't want to see. Oh no, there was a PA State Trooper who decided to pull me over. I was very impressed with his patrol car. It had blue, white, and red flashing lights. The trooper car was white with some kind of writing on it. (Why do law enforcement folks always have white autos and those charming lights affixed atop?) The reason I didn't get a good look at the writing on his car was it was parked right behind me, so I only saw his front end. As I was swallowing hard, my brain already knew what he was going to say. He had the gall to tell me I was going 67 mph in a 55 mph zone. I suppose part of the game is to act surprised, that really we didn't know that fact. What I don't understand: why do police people keep their red, white, and blue flashing lights on after they catch us? It is so embarrassing. What will all those other motorists think of me? I've done something bad, and I got caught at it. (The key is you can do something bad; just don't get caught at it.) Besides his flashing lights, I was impressed by his speed detecting device and his video camera that filmed the whole dastardly affair. (If I knew I was being filmed, I would have spruced up a bit.) Yes, I know I was speeding (damn't), officer. My next approach was to make all kinds of excuses for my breaking the law. (I guess I found a rule I shouldn't have broken.) Step three was to engage the state trooper in humor. (I'm still trying to figure out whether I was manipulating the state trooper or was I just being me?) I don't remember the trooper's name. He not only told me up front what it was, his name was on a black badge with white letters on his chest as well. For the life of me, I can't remember it. It was probably because I was very fearful about being caught. I blanked it out. I will call him officer Breien. This officer Breien was attired in a sorta light gray uniform. His hat was especially cool, but I don't think it was very comfortable to wear. Every time he got into his fancy car, he took it off. He didn't put it on again until he strolled towards my bad car. And officer Breien had that frightening black pad in his hands. Since I grew up with a heavy dose of respecting all authority figures, I was agreeable and demur. (At least I knew he wasn't going to bat me around in an angry rage.) When he finally came back to my car with his black pad, I asked him what my fee would be and what the punishment would be. He was very professional, very aware of the PA laws and my civil rights. Another good thing—trooper Breien was cute. All during this time, I was trying to have fun with officer Breien. He was sorta laughing behind his official MO. You are not going to believe this: He only gave me a warning and advised me to slow down in the future. Perhaps he thought I was cute? Could it have been that I am a senior citizen? I can't answer these questions, so I'll just chalk it up to luck. His final words to me were, "Be careful getting back on the highway." (The question remains—was I being my engaging self or trying to manipulate state trooper Breien???)

Now I'm thinking what could I write about.

"We are all on the highway of life, going at different mph's."

"There are those who travel in the fast lane and those parked on the shoulder."

I think I could dream up a whole bunch of motorist metaphors. Would that make you puke? How trite and corny could I be? How much of this make believe could you stomach? I do have some fairy dust at home I could mail to you. If only it could help us become who we truly are and help us to embrace life with gusto.

I could have written corny things. I came from a direct lineage of the house of David. (David was my dad's name.) We—my mom, two sisters, and I—believed dad had a gift for corn. He was knighted by QE2, or was it King George? He was tapped on the shoulders with the traditional sword and thereby he became the "royal highness of corn man." There were real fancy words that went with the ceremony. They were blah, blah, blah, and now my dad had all the "rights and privileges thereof." We became dad's living audience. We would fake our enjoyment by half-baked giggles and "ohoooos." We even used a fancy word, "two shay." I'm not sure I spelled that right. It is a foreign word and foreign words are foreign to me. (I didn't do well with foreign languages, either. Come to think about it, I don't know what I did well in at school.) Since we reacted the same every time dad was corny, he got even cornier. I think he liked the attention. It became a drag to hear corn after corn after corn. How do we get out of this game? We never found an answer to that question. Dad was corny, almost to the end. He really took his "sirhood of corn" very seriously. The only problem was, he didn't know when to give it up or when to call it a day. He was cocky and confident that we found him funny. He was so corny some weeks, we had enough corn for suppers to come. (And we didn't live in Iowa.) Just because it sounds like corn doesn't mean you want to eat it for supper. The sad thing was, dad didn't realize his corn was actually put-downs and not funny at all. I'm sure you can see how hard it would be to grow up being made fun of; that dad's corn was really at our expense. You know, the more I think about it, there are plenty of people who still use humor that seems funny on one level but is hurtful to others. I probably shouldn't say this, but sometimes we thought dad was farting. No class, right? Would it help if I used "passing gas"? Would it be in better taste? Eventually we would hold our noses and swish our hands at the same time, a gesture to suggest we were trying to rid the room of the smell from all that foul corn—like he had dropped a gas bomb. We all felt embarrassed for dad when he was farting around. We were embarrassed for him because his corn was almost as bad as his farting around. They were equally smelly.

Can you tell me how while I'm pushing my Hoover vac, the cord gets completely wrapped around my ankle? It's like I've been lassoed, hog tied, and down for the count. I bet you are asking yourselves, "What does this have to do with the rest of this letter?" It doesn't.

With my dad's corn, it was better than his prejudices. He was anti-everything that wasn't like himself. He was anti—nationalities, race, ethnic groups, religious denominations, and any other perversions he deemed to be abominations. All this came out in his corn and wise cracks. He actually expected others to "pull themselves up by their own boot straps." I hate to tell you, dad, but it can't be done. I felt embarrassed for my dad when he took his bigotry on the road.

Worse than my dad's corn and bigotry were his violent rages. We never knew what would set him off. Consequently, my two sisters and I lived with fear and apprehension all the time. My father's humongous venom and anger spewed onto us kids. (And it didn't even stop when we were older kids.) He lashed out at us with screaming and hitting. There was no place to hide. I kept asking myself, "What awful thing did I do to deserve this wrath?" His incidents were often and long in duration. He was out of control. There were nights he would come into reiny's and my bedroom and strike us both for no apparent reason. Only he knew. There were many nights my silent tears ran down into my ears and dampened my pillow.

And the tragedy of all these happenings—I never learned how to express my anger in appropriate and healthy ways, so I didn't. Then it happened. All my fears came to fruition. With years and years of storing my anger in my gut, one day my arsenal of anger exploded. I blew. I blasted. My anger was splattered on walls, ceilings, floors. I fell apart. I had a meltdown. I imploded. I freaked. I was one big ball of rage like dad.

Paradoxically, my plummet into the abyss was the beginning of my willing and not-so-willing attempts to sort through the crippling, destructive, and defeating aspects of my life. And, dad, I did it in spite of you!

At this point, let me assure you I'm not a romantic or an idealist. I'm not about thinking we will live happily ever after, nor apple pie in the sky, nor bye and bye. My empowerment was an arduous path that took hard work and years of processing for physical and mental well-being. The road was never a straight line. It was circular. It zigzagged. Emotionally I was bouncing up and down. All my mixed-up feelings and thoughts overwhelmed me. They came unexpectedly, but repeatedly, and it took all of my energy to revisit the pain. The task was intense, and many times I said, "The hell with *this*." As you know with your own inner struggles, the pilgrimage never ends till it ends. But in the here and now, our voyage could be joined, linked, so together we can share what being human is all about. Let's partake of our matchless gifts to hook up, heart to heart, soul to soul. Life is always evolving, and we never stop learning. Some of us lucky ones were able to find "personal trainers" who helped us to search, were there for us in the valleys and the heights, cheered us on when the going got tough, and cheered even when we were in a good place. They helped us find our epiphanies and gave caring support, sometimes holding our hands, even giving hugs, helping us find some rest from the trek, and even succor from the pain. I have been blessed by my soulful presence in my life. Mike was the spark that stoked my imagination to begin writing my letters, and you know the rest. Even if you have not had a professional help you through life, we can help to heal each other. We have that power. Let's do it! We don't always need a medicine man, but we can pass the peace pipe, adorned with ribbons, feathers, beads, and strips of rawhide, all in vibrant colors. What ya say?

The only time I saw my dad's soul was when he listened to music. Tears would run down his face, without any embarrassment on his part. I had always wished I could have tapped his other hidden feelings, all those marvelous feelings he held hidden inside himself. I sure hope you will allow your feelings to surface. You know, you won't lose control of them if you do. Believe me, you don't have to be dragged into an ambulance and taken to the loony bin to figure out that denying our feelings hurts us. I came to find out that swallowing my feelings—fixing the problem by making myself numb, detached, and out of touch with reality—made me sick. I learned that by feeling and expressing my feelings, I could mend. I had to do the reverse of eating. I had to vomit up all that was making me ill—my locked-away feelings and my lost soul. I just didn't know my way to that promised land. I had many guides though. My point being, if we don't look inside for those feelings, we will not find our soul, either. We have all been given a limitless supply of spirit. If we don't (or won't) take that trip inwardly, we will miss out on the greatest gift of all: the gift of life. And one size fits all. You won't ever have to return it for your correct size. It is a priceless treasure I would not suggest you store in your safe deposit boxes. Let us get in line with all those other souls to find, experience, share, and then rejoice in all the beauty and awe that surrounds us, that holds us tight. You see, my dad held on tight to his soul. He believed there wouldn't be enough to go around. It wouldn't last, so he had to hoard it. "Unknown readers," I hope you don't allow yourselves to feel only on special occasions, like my dad. Are we so afraid of that? I'm still sad that my dad died without ever knowing or living from his soul. Let us find the voice for our souls.

I'm coming to the end of this letter, and I'm hoping you haven't been telling yourself, "This letter is *awfully* long. Reading it is like having quadruple bypass surgery, without the anesthesia." But I want to ask you in your reading of it, do you come to the same conclusion I did? That to find our soul within, we need to find our child within also? Our child of wonderment, trust, curiosity, hope…the child who sees no limits, just exciting possibilities.

only being 1 host, (there are many more) I'm inviting you to join with me at the feast of soul and new life

to an unknown funeral director—

Oh no! Oh, my god! Holy cow! State Trooper Breien has cloned himself. I see him all over the place. He still has that boring white official car with the same white, blue, and red flashing lights. Obviously he still has his radar gun. How else would he be able to clock his prey? If he didn't have his radar gun, he would be out of a job. I've seen him standing tall by opened windows requesting all those official papers we hide in our glove compartments, which we don't have our gloves in. Today I saw Officer Breien with his whole body halfway into the window of a pulled-over driver, nose to nose, like he was trying to be up front and personal. Thank God he didn't do that to me. I have problems with boundaries, especially when they are invaded. Maybe the driver didn't respect authority figures like I did. Perhaps they were duking it out. I don't think he was being a good "victim" of Trooper Breien. Victims don't usually fight back. So beware, State Trooper Breien is everywhere. I don't know about you, but I'm feeling paranoid right about now. I know for sure Trooper Breien has a mission. He is out to get us. Just wanted to warn you.

I guess I should get to the salutation above, unless you have already said, "You can count me out." I suppose the topic is not a very popular one to read about or even to think about. Well, I'm sorry to say, I'm going with it. It might be a hoot to you "unknown readers." I just hope I don't offend you, but I guess that is your choice.

My most favorite funeral director was Doug. Unfortunately, I knew him quite well. His funeral home arranged the details of dying for many. Another way I knew him was every time I had surgery (which seemed excessive), he was very caring and sent me flowers and china bowls full of all kinds of plants. Have you ever heard of a funeral director doing such a thing? He sure spent a lot of money on me since I was a patient so many times. I was in need of tons of cheer. I just realized I'm an organ donor, but with so many surgeries, I don't have many organs left. I guess it would be a good idea to remove that phrase from my driver's license so they wouldn't have false hopes. The process of getting a procedure done starts with those alarming symptoms, which brings our problem right to the fore. Then there are all those doc. visits (which are a pain in the neck). More delays. Then we have to endure all those absurd diagnostic tests that were ordered by our doc. More delays. How long do I have to be in agony? My condition was greatly improved when I was under, feeling no pain. It wasn't till after the successful operation I felt like crap. I was told I can expect four to six weeks to fully recover. Tell me, in what medical journal does it say that magical number of four to six weeks until we patients feel our old selves again? Maybe it's from Socrates' time? Or does it have something to do with that Hippocratic Oath thing? "Do no harm." Yeah, give me a break. I'm not that ignorant. Your "do no harm" is a crock. Look, you did do harm. I'm missing organs. I'm feeling lousy, and I will for those four to six weeks more. "Do no harm." Look at my scars. I certainly don't look as I did when I came into this world. Then the ob-gyn said I was perfect. I'm not about to show anyone the criss-crossings all over my old body—those incisions and scars (at least all my scars match). They will never let us forget those stinking happenings in our lives.

Doug also knew that "Hippocratic Oath" wasn't to be taken seriously either. He sent those gifts because he knew I had been harmed, although sometimes I wondered if the flowers and plants he sent were to keep a future customer happy. The only drawback to receiving all this cheer—I had to write all those damn "thank you" notes. Please don't get me wrong. I have always written "thank you" notes to people who have shown their kindness to me. Then there were all those "thank you" notes I had to write to church members who sent us gifts of food as well. Can you imagine how many "thank you" notes that means? It's really hard to be clever time after time. Besides, the recipients might compare notes. Do you know how many words there are to say thanks? Zip! Nada! Let's have a contest to see who can come up with some new, exciting thank-you words. (No foreign words, that's cheating.) I'll even throw in a free paid trip to Outer Macedonia for the winner.

Doug would call the parsonage to inform Dave that there had been a death and to ask him if he would be available to do the service. I would ask Doug, "Is it one of ours?" In retrospect, that question was very arrogant of me. Like the "ours" were only important. Only *our* loved ones' deaths mattered. By saying those words, I was discounting that we all grieve and mourn our dead. Every life that departs from us is a loss to someone. We are all in the same dying and death journey. None of us will outlive death. We are the "ours." Eventually we will be seeing that funeral director, or the old term, the undertaker. It's pretty clear to me that the funeral director directs and the undertaker takes us under. I don't think I have to go into detail about the rest of the process once the funeral director takes over. We all know. We all have experienced these sad times in our lives.

One thing I don't understand—why is the color of choice black for these horrendous affairs? Is it from the black plague that was deadly? Or could it possibly have come from somewhere in human history? Maybe, at one point, black was so chic, so "in," that everyone was dying to wear it. The only thing I know that black is great for—it makes the wearer look skinnier. I can't wear black. With my fair skin, it makes me look half alive, ghostly. I don't think black should even be on the color chart, but I'm not sure it is anyway. Right?

Does the death of our loved ones give us pause to think about the serious questions of where we are in the time we have left? I would think that all the funerals we have attended in our lifetime would be a wakeup call for us. That by death, we have a chance to do something about our living. Remember, before that funeral director/undertaker comes to get us, let's live our lives to the brim. We can make a decision to live our lives to the max. May our grieving and mourning of our losses help us to know we still have time to feel and savor our aliveness. Will we let ourselves learn the lessons from our dead? They have a lot to teach us from the grave. Are we listening to their pleading voices? They are telling us we don't have forever on this planet. Everything is measured in time. How much time do we have? No one can answer that question, but since life is open-ended, let's live before we die. We certainly don't want to wake up some morning and find ourselves dead. I think we might have regrets as to what we had missed in our living. Life is limited, so may our lives be enriched for this one day. It's all we have. Are we ready to assess our lives? Can we get out from under our own funeral palls, trade them in for a glimmering robe with opals, amethysts, and other precious stones? Put a crown upon our heads with studded ropes of pearls? Now we are bedecked with empowerment, hope, and courage. With these attributes, we can celebrate our lives's novel and diverse routes. We are in charge. Only we can change those things in our lives that are suffocating us, causing us to feel like we are dying. Let's raise our filled glasses to make a toast to all the beautiful and awesome things in our lives: "Hear! Hear!"

How about another round of that fantastic gift? "Hear! Hear!"

think about joining me in the pilgrimage of our life's time

tell me, what will it be?

to an unknown future—

"What?" you might be asking. "How can she write about something neither she nor we know anything about? This is dumb. We know she is an old lady. Could she have dementia?"

You are right in asking how I can write a letter about the future. I have no erudite, brilliant thing to say about the topic. I'm not a future teller, not even a soothsayer, nor a crystal globe watcher. It's an oxymoron—if I attempt to write about the future, the future will become the here and now. We have enough trouble staying in the present. We often try to fluctuate back to the past and try to skip into the unknown future. How many of you "unknown readers," myself included, actually live in the present? We think we live in the present, but how much of our past histories do we drag into our nows? And how can we love and embrace life if we are stuck in the past and worrying about the future? We only have power in our existing times, yet we don't always have control. We can anticipate, plan for the future, but we are impotent in mastery over it. Maybe having the knowledge we can't rule the future lends to our feelings of vulnerability. And feeling susceptible and vulnerable sucks. We want to have dominion over our destinies, but we need to come to the realization that we can only live in the moment. All we have are our todays. Let's not be paralyzed in our present days by focusing on the past or the future. Tell me, can we hold hands as we rejoice into the process of time?

a fable

In the fall, have you seen those geese flying in their V formations? I don't think you could miss them—they make a ton of noise as they fly above us mortals. There is always a lead goose, with all the other birds streaming behind. When the leader gets weary, he drops back into the flock and another goose takes the first position. If one of the geese is injured or is going to die, he flies down to the earth to end his flocking journey. But a beautiful thing happens—two other geese fly down to join him in his agony, to comfort him in his end-time process. After giving solace, they leave their beloved dead goose behind, and then the two geese fly back into the heavens to catch up with all the other travelers in their familiar V formations.

Can we be so connected in our per diems?

will you fly with me in a V formation?
from one goose to another goose

to an unknown mother—

I'm sure you are asking yourselves, "How can a mother be unknown?"
It may not be true for you, but in my life it was. You were lucky to
have had a relationship with a *known* mother —you knew she loved
you. You knew you could trust that she would be there for you. You
knew that you were the most important thing in her life.

You knew her hugs were limitless. You knew you didn't have to
earn her love. You knew she would push your swing as high as it could
go. You knew she would understand that playing was a big deal to a kid.
You knew she realized imaginary friends were really real and even had
names. She could see all the magical things in your world were really
real. You knew she could see a lacy spider web with droplets of dew, in
all its beauty, without having seen the spider. You knew she knew your
sandcastle at the shore was going to be washed away by a foamy wave
and helped you to take it in gleeful stride, as you could build another
one anyway. You knew she would teach you about a loving God. You
knew she knew weeping willows do, in fact, cry. You knew she knew
frogs didn't really cause warts. It was okay to hold them, if you could
catch them. You knew she would let you sit in her lap for eternity. You
knew she would let you find your own path to travel. You knew she
would once in a while let you win at tiddly winks. You knew she would
keep you safe. You knew she would help you with all the scary things
in your kid world. You knew she would let you be anything you wanted

to be when you grew up, and it was okay to keep changing your mind. You knew she was okay with your believing that there really was a man in the moon whom you could say goodnight to. You knew she would encourage you to see beyond your own backyard. She loved to give you gifts. You knew she didn't care if you sang silly songs or said silly things. You knew she could handle that crocuses sometimes pop up in the snow. You knew she understood that everything had to be fast in a kid's life. You knew she would help you figure things out in your world. You knew she believed learning wasn't just at school but wherever, forever. You knew she wasn't going to get angry when you got dirty while playing. You knew she would teach you the rules of life. You knew she loved your father, too. You knew she saw you, and everyone else for that matter, as unique, different, and special. You knew she knew where leprechauns live. You knew, even when a new baby came along, you were just as important as ever to her. You knew she would be with you for bedtime prayers. You knew she would be straight with you—no secrets. You knew she would respect your space. You knew she would say fun is more than okay. She knew it didn't matter if your room was a bit messy; that there was time for cleaning up another day. You knew she would accept others regardless of their wrapping paper. You knew she wasn't interested in impressing or competing with other people. You knew she would find the smell of low tide beautiful. You knew she would encourage you to just be you. You knew she would use summer, fall, winter, and spring to teach you about life's cycles. You knew she knew there were no two snowflakes alike, and snow tasted best with maple syrup on it. You knew she couldn't figure out why high mountains are one with the sky, nor figure out where one began or ended either, just like you. You knew she would try to answer all your persistent questions without getting mad. You knew she knew how hippopotamuses talk. You knew she knew her parents were fantastic grandparents so you could too.

You knew she knew that sometimes your heart can break. You knew she would play ring-around-the-rosy with you for always. You knew she wouldn't freak when you spilled grape Kool-aid on the rug. You knew she knew thunderstorms weren't the end of the world, merely one of God's shows. You knew even if you did something bad, she wasn't going to hit you with anything she could get her hands on. You knew she also knew silence is beautiful. You knew she knew that Santa really didn't judge kids as either bad or good; he just brought joy. You knew she knew that ugly, black, green, crawling things will really turn into fantastic multi-colored butterflies; you just had to be patient. You knew she wouldn't be upset when ice cream from your cone melted all down your hands and arms, or worse, the whole scoop fell on the ground. You knew she knew where the sun went to sleep. You knew she knew why black and yellow bumble bees hum. You knew she knew why God made poison ivy, boa constrictors, armadillos, horseshoe crabs, and jelly fish. You knew she knew your first time for doing some things was so marvelous. You knew she knew that things don't always have to be what they seem to be. You knew she would read your favorite bed-time stories over and over. You knew she knew how to find you if you lost your way. You knew she could tell you how yucky tasting medicine was good for you, and you believed her. You knew she knew laughing could grow and grow and grow since there was no end to it. You knew she could tell you why tumbleweeds tumble. You knew she could tell you why mosquitoes wear lipstick. You knew she understood that brothers and sisters fighting was a fact of life. You knew that she knew yelling really, really hurt your ears. You knew that she knew the toll collector wasn't going to collect you for a ride on his road. You knew she would show you how red bleeding hearts bleed little white drops, not crimson. You knew she knew that the sole reason for mushrooms was to be umbrellas for pixies. You knew she knew how magical your magic markers really were. You knew she knew reading was a precious gift because words were so awesome. You knew she believed just because you were a kid didn't mean you were wrong all the time. You knew when she told you to close your eyes tight and open them again, there really would be a wonderful surprise. You knew she knew when you were very excited, it was hard to be patient. You knew she knew that raccoons really weren't bandits and wouldn't steal from you. You knew she knew that forget-me-nots really do remember. You knew she would teach you when you used a screwdriver, turning it right or left made all the difference in the world. You knew she understood sometimes there doesn't have to be a reason for everything, some things just are. You knew she knew sometimes it was okay to cry. You knew she knew why a falling star's lamp would go out. You knew she knew why water in different places made different sounds. You knew she knew how all those little yellow flowers in everyone's yards turned into fabulous white fluffy things with black seeds you could blow. You knew she knew how your glass of milk could become part of the Milky Way. You knew she could tell you why lemons weren't always sour. You knew she could tell you why your soda fizzed (and it wasn't because of the seltzer). You knew she understood being a kid, you could never get enough of a good thing. You knew she wasn't going to violate your little body. You knew she would let you decorate gingerbread men cookies, from head to toe, anyway you wanted. You knew she could tell you stories about all the living creatures that once lived in the discarded shells at the seashore. You knew she knew when to say she was sorry. You knew she knew that kisses fixed everything. You knew she would teach you that doing work, tasks, or chores weren't the only things important about life. You knew that she could convince you there really were good witches. You knew she would teach you how to tie your sneaker laces and understood it would take lots of practice. You knew she knew who was so smart to have invented your soft, cuddly, beloved bed pillow that smelled like sleep. You knew she would encourage you to dare to explore your planet. You knew she knew what the word "autonomy" meant. You knew she believed sometimes your walk left behind indelible marks on others' hearts.

If you had a mother like this, you were so lucky.

from an unknown daughter

to a known...

It happened again. Once again, my soulful presence brought up an idea that I might want to consider writing what might be one last letter. The topic he mentioned was to write about myself me. He said something I didn't understand: that it might be good for me to be able to give myself credit for having a "good" soul, that by writing this letter I could share with my "unknown readers" an inward reflection and discovery, and by doing so, I could then own my own "good" qualities. (How boring for you.) Writing this suggested sort of letter may be intended to increase my self-esteem (an overused, hackneyed phrase of our pop culture); it's just not what myself me is willing to pen.

Prior to my conversation with mike, I had already decided that my last letter was going to be "to an unknown mother." My first reaction to writing a letter to myself me triggered those old messages in my head I have tried to silence all these years:

"What, the letters I've written aren't good enough?"

"Do I have to meet mike's expectations?"

"Do I need to agree with his notion?"

"Do I have to please him by forgetting my needs?"

"And if I don't do it his way, will he love me less?"

"Can I successfully write yet another letter?"

"I already know it will be impossible to create."

"I know I will fail."

"I don't think I have any inspiration left in me."

Every letter I've written, I've thought it was the most difficult, but this letter proposal is throwing me. I'm not going to do this one, mike or no mike.

In all the time mike and I have shared together, have been able to create a deeper relationship, how could he even suggest this project? He knows full well I'm not into "meism." My M.O. is one of humility, unassuming and unpretentious. My lifestyle has focused on others. I try to be aware of others' needs—try to understand, and try to give support, to connect with them. In doing so, I engage in the commonness of us all. I continue to invite us to merge with one another so we may tramp on for dignity, justice, responsibility, and peace, and crush evil on the earth. There is where we will find our uniqueness and likenesses and a common soul, as we enter our own tour of duty. More important than our preoccupation with what we will do today, how our future will play out, is our passage inwardly. Something good will happen to us. The unexpected will happen. Wonders, you find, will never cease. Do we have the courage and passion to accomplish this?

Well, my "unknown readers," you already know I'm not writing this "me" letter, but I'll say it again: I'm not writing this "me" letter. You already know me. Who I am, how I write, what I write about, what I share, has been there for you to see in my letters. I'm the soul behind the words. You will find myself me there. It's my gift to you, "unknown readers." The rest is up to you. You can open my gift with thanks, or you can put my book of letters back on Barnes & Nobles' bookshelf. It's your call. It's up to you guys.

A story to share with you —

A man (or woman) was running down a path in the bush, being chased by a snow leopard. He ran and ran in the wild with great fear and great effort to escape with his life. As he exerted himself to outrun the grayish-white, irregularly blotched beast of prey, he came to the trail's end. At that point, he realized he was facing a plunge over the cliff onto the unyielding piles of rocks below. What now? Either he would be eaten alive by the fast-approaching, menacing predator or fall to his death at the bottom of the ravine. As he was tottering on the edge, he temporarily found himself perched on a branch. It was then he discovered a strawberry bush growing there. As he hung in the balance, he took a strawberry, ate it, and said, "This is the best strawberry I've ever tasted."

life is a mystery

to an unknown end—

Is it going to be, "That's all folks?" Right now, I don't have an ending place. As I have done in the past, when I finish a letter, I say to myself, "This is definitely the last one." If I stop with this letter, I'm concerned about what I will do with myself if I'm not writing letters. I sure don't feel like washing the fridge again—seems like I just did that. What do I do with my passion to write letters? Life bombards my senses and intellect, which I hastily put down on paper. The thoughts, sights, sounds, and smells around me become ideas to share with you readers. What do I do with my creative energy if I stop writing? Writing has given me a rush, a high—and you know we junkies need our fixes daily. Maybe I don't have any imagination left in me; maybe my inspiration is gone. Maybe I don't have the right (write) stuff anymore. Maybe the final curtain will rain down on the "unknown writer." Maybe the well is dry. Maybe I should say enough is enough. Perhaps what I have already written is as much as I am going to write? Perhaps I've come to the end? But how will I know?

I know life ends, but if you believe in the resurrection, it doesn't. Schools close for summer break, but kids go back in the fall. There is an unfinished symphony. A bestseller comes to an end (unless you read the last chapter first), but there are bound to be sequels to come. As long as we keep winding our clocks, they will run forever—unless they break. Then we will buy another one that continues to click as long as

60

we keep winding it. It takes a long time to put out forest fires, but we know there will be more to come. Our buying and collecting stuff will never end. Indulging ourselves won't end—it will only grow. Perennials die, but we know there is new life to come hidden underground. May there always be a "moon river." The ocean will never end, but it might swell to such proportions as to flood our coastal lands. A lit candle will be blown out, but we can rekindle it. We can even melt down the candle's last remains and make a new one. I remember going to Nantucket and seeing homes and villages going back to the 1770s. The people died, but their possessions were on display, telling us things will outlive us. My marriage ended, but now we are better friends. When our loved ones die, our memories of them go on and on. When we listen to music on our radios, the songs might end, but we can change the channel to hear more tunes. Our hair doesn't stop growing unless we are bald—then it did stop. We know the moon and the sun alternate their appearances in the sky, but we also trust this pattern will continue till the very end of time. Hugs don't have endings. There is always hope for more to come our way tomorrow. Fighting for justice and freedom should never end. Wars never end. There is a war going on someplace on our planet. Love is for always. Our souls never perish. Melodies linger on in our heads. May there be no end to the heaps and heaps of blessings we receive. Man's search for meaning never stops. Our faith walk evolves—we would never want to close the book on our spirituality. Sometimes I wonder if my earthly pilgrimage will end in a nursing home. What will the end be like? Will dying be cruel? When we finish our scrambled eggs, we know that trusty hens will drop more of those white or brown eggs. It's amazing how many things in our lives reassure us life goes on and on and on and on…there is always the possibility for renewal.

May all the "helpers" out there never stop sharing themselves and their gifts towards new life for us seekers. We can't change salt from being salt or pepper from being pepper—it will always be that way. My shredder ends my paper's life. We have learned about earlier geological ages through our finds of petrified fossils. Tell me, are those fossils alive or dead? Baby swans are born with ugly brown feathers, but they become elegant, long-necked, soft-white swans and live out the rest of their lives with dignity and splendor. My victimhood has ended, but my newfound life is awesome. Reiny, debbie, and I have gotten really close now in spite of our childhood. When we smell rose buds, they have such a delicate fragrance. They wither and die, but we know next spring we will be able to repeat our rapture with them. Our civilization will never end for there will be kids after kids to carry society forward—but I feel for the kids who will witness the end of time. Man's creative genius lives on. Children will never stop loving being read to. Volcanoes won't stop belching fire and red and black lava, but sometimes they sleep a long while. God's peace and love never ends. We may finish reading a book, but there are limitless numbers more to read. I wish my toenails would stop growing—it's a pain to have to cut them; they are so hard to reach. Sometimes friendships end, but that is because we are human, and that will never change. Most everyone ends their working careers by retiring, but they become overjoyed to be able to explore all the new vistas there are for their lives. Tooth decay dies when we go to the dentist, but that's a good thing. There is no end to housework. Being computer-disabled, I think it is safe to say computers have short lives.

May we always give thanks. May we continue to have lofty ideals. May there always be a "sea of tranquility." Let's die to sin every day. I hope lies will eventually cease. There is an end cycle on my washing machine, but we both know it will start from the beginning to end again on the next washday. The Christmas season ends, but not the message. Sadness can end when laughter comes on the scene. May we never kill our joy and rejoicing. History is a living entity. Bugs crawl into my house. I wish *they* would die. Then there are the words—"All's well that ends well." I sure wished my colonoscopy would have ended sooner. Man's intellect surpasses time. I'm not ready for my life to end just yet. I wish gossip and pettiness would drop dead. I wish bad memories would take a hike. There is so much beauty and awe on our spinning globe. I sure wouldn't want that to end. I'm so glad my periods stopped. Shells on the beach may be crushed, but their fragments are still shells. The race to develop technology will never end. I pray tolerance for diversity will never die. We are already facing a water crisis, and that could be the end of our way of life as we know it. Our natural resources are dwindling, but we can take responsibility to ensure that doesn't continue. When our pets die, perhaps in time, we replace them with another loveable animal. May there always be a star to wish upon. "We can't go home again." It will never be the same as when we were growing up.

Phew! Ohhh-kay, now what? Writing all this hasn't helped me one bit. How do I answer my own question? Is this letter going to be my swan song? In my letters, I ask a lot of questions. Sometimes they are rhetorical—no answers required. However, my question to myself needs an answer. I guess my last question in this letter is, "Will I write any more letters to you, my 'unknown readers'?" In my day, the answer to a question was, "Only the phantom knows." I wish there could be a way to take a vote to help me decide. But my question can't be answered by results of any straw poll; not even a public opinion poll would help. What makes it even tougher is that I don't like making *big* decisions. They scare me. Of course, some decisions are weightier than others. This question is gigantic for me. I also have to factor in what others' expectations might be for me. I really don't know how to end this letter. Well, that isn't entirely true. I know how to end the letter. I just don't know how to end this letter with an answer to my question. Sometimes we make a decision by not deciding. In the past, when I couldn't make a decision, I would pout, stamp my feet, cross my arms, and run out of the room crying and screaming. Obviously it didn't work then, so it certainly isn't going to work now. I don't have the Internet for serious research. What's the question again? Wait a sec. I just figured out how to solve my problem. To make my decision, I have to journey inside to sort out my thoughts and feelings. To find my answer is more than a head trip. Spreadsheets won't cut it. The answer I'm seeking will only come from my soul's soft voice. I just have to listen. In this letter, the majority of my words speak to continuations, but aren't there times in the scheme of things when some endings prove necessary?

life is a mystery,
lovebye

Appendix

obit

to an unknown newspaper—

Grace Evangelin Cote, age ____, of Selinsgrove, PA, died [when and where].- Born in Brooklyn, NY, she was the daughter of the late Grace M. and David R. Breien. She is survived by three children: Rebekkah Anne, Bynum, NC; Paul David, Richfield, PA; and Mark David, West Chester, PA; four grandchildren: Katherine Grace and Mary Helen of Richfield; Matthew David and Sarah Elizabeth of West Chester; sisters: Reinholdine Breien Pierson, and her husband, Leonard, Virginia Beach, VA; and Deborah Rebekka Breien, South Weymouth, MA; several nieces and nephews, and her ex-husband, The Rev. David R. Cote, Gardner, MA.

Grace accomplished many things in her life, including educational and vocational achievements. She embraced doing charitable works. Her faith journey was nurtured in several Lutheran churches in New England. She continually thanked God for blessing her life with the gifts of Rebekkah; Paul, his wife, Patty, Katie and Mary; Mark, his wife, Linda, Matthew and Sarah. There are no adequate words of thanks for all the human beings that touched her life. She wants to be remembered for her laughter, her intellect, her joy in life's experiences, her forbearance in suffering, and her compassionate soul, and as a published author of Letters from "an unknown writer."

There are no calling hours. Her funeral service will be held [date, time, name of church, address] with Rev. [name] officiating. Interment will follow in [name of cemetery]. Immediately following the committal service, a celebration party for Grace's life will be held at [name, address, phone number].

In lieu of flowers, the family requests contributions be sent to Geisinger Health System, MC 40-00, 100 North Academy Avenue, Danville, PA 17822-3941 (RE: Mental Health Outpatient Services); The American Cancer Society, Central Susquehanna, 57 Reitz Boulevard, Suite 102, Lewisburg, PA 17837; National Fragile X Foundation, PO Box 190488, San Francisco, CA 94119-0488; or a local hospice [name and address].

Arrangements by [funeral home, name and phone number].